AMERICA'S
OPPORTUNITIES

BY JAMES A. NELSON

ISBN: 1492111910
ISBN-13: 9781492111917
Library of Congress Control Number: 2013914882
CreateSpace Independent Publishing Platform
North Charleston, South Carolina

I pledge allegiance to the flag of the United States of America, and to the republic for which it stands, one nation under God, indivisible, with liberty and justice for all.

BUDDY NELSON'S HANGAR is as big
as man's imagination. There are no locks
on the doors and the only membership
requirements are Curiosity, Faith, Desire
and Determination.

INTRODUCTION

My Editor Ms. Bessie, my gorgeous wife Marylil, and my two wonderful children Sabryna and Darrick thought *"America's Opportunities"* was too harsh and strident in tone to be included as an "Afterword" in my book *'ROCK HILL.'* They all felt it would destroy the readers' enjoyment of *"Jim's Story."* My simple point was to compare America then with America now: perhaps they were correct; let the reader be the Judge.

My wife and I also disagreed over the title for this book. She preferred: *"Opportunities In America."* I said my point with the title *"America's Opportunities"* was that **All American Citizens**, not just the top one, two, three or even 20 per cent of the population; not just lobbyists and politicians in Washington D.C.; but **All American Citizens** must step forward to make their positions known through the Ballot Box and other forms of Lawful Expression.

DEDICATION

TO MY FELLOW AMERICANS
Especially
My Wife, Children and Grandson

ACKNOWLEDGMENTS

I would like to acknowledge a few special people who were instrumental in the creation of this book. **FIRST:** My wife, Marylil, who started out as "Clerk Typist," then promoted herself first to "Editor" and finally to "Writer" as the copy returned totally changed from what I thought I had written. She said "Oh, but I believe my changes read a little better." **SECOND:** my daughter Vanessa Nelson-McCalister who saved *America's Opportunities* on her computer until I finally decided to finish this work. **THIRD:** Ms. Cathy Pedigo from the State of Kentucky, a gorgeous woman who is a whiz on the keyboard, extremely intelligent and a Precious Friend I shall cherish forever. **FOURTH:** my very talented son Tyrone Nelson who with his professional computer skills e-mailed the manuscript in a Word document to the publisher and helped his parents with the IT (Self-Publishing) challenges.

I would also like to thank my "LISTENERS" - - those respected Loved Ones, Dear Friends, and Esteemed Associates who listened to some of what I had written. The listing of their names does not mean that any or all agreed with my writing: Ms. Sabryna Bach, Mr. Albert E. Carter, Ms. Tonya Chapman, Mr. Clifford Clark, Mr. and Mrs. Tom and Lucy Fullerton, Ms. Christine Hassing, Ms. Betty Hess, Mr. Jim Honke, Ms. Patricia Johnson, Ms. Patricia Martin, Mr. Jeff McCalister, Mrs. Vanessa Nelson-McCalister, Mrs.Vivian Mohns, Mr. Darrick Nelson, Mrs. Marylil Nelson, Mr. Tyrone Nelson, Mr. Robert Nordlie, Ms. Cathy Pedigo, Mr. Howard L. Phillips, Attorney at Law, Mrs. Louise Pruitt, Ms. Nancy Richards, Ms. Mary Jo Sato, Ms. Elsie Simmons, Mr. Dick Stiles, Mrs. Laura Walter, Ms. Catherine Waters, Mr. Jerry Weible, Mrs. Jewell Wells and Mr. James M. Womack, Attorney at Law.

SPECIAL NOTE

When I think of the condition of my Country today, I remember reading what President Abraham Lincoln said in 1862: When asked how he felt about a New York State Gubernatorial Race being won by a Democratic candidate, President Lincoln replied: "Somewhat like the boy in Kentucky, who stubbed his toe while running to see his sweetheart. The boy said he was too old to cry, and hurt too badly to laugh!"

TABLE OF CONTENTS

"There is nothing new in the world except the history you do not Know."

President Harry S. Truman

MEMORABLE SPEECHES
FIVE STAR GENERAL
DOUGLAS MacARTHUR
RABBI JOACHIM PRINZ
US REPRESENTATIVE BARBARA LEE
US SENATOR ROBERT BYRD
AND
PRESIDENTS PAST

BUDDY NELSON'S HANGAR *is as big
as man's imagination. There are no locks
on the doors and the only membership
requirements are Curiosity, Faith, Desire
and Determination.*

Dear Sabryna, Darrick, Vanessa, Tyrone, Tyler and my Fellow Americans:

My *"Rock Hill"* Story was lived many years ago. Since then I have witnessed my beloved Country change in ways that are both unbelievable and disappointing. Life's values that many of my Teachers taught us have unfortunately gone by the wayside. During the 1940's and 1950's, The United States was respected and envied the world over for our democratic government, military power, and generosity to others. Jobs were plentiful, incomes were high and America's future looked unlimited. Yes, there was atrocious racial discrimination but our Country was working on solutions, however slowly. Today, my Country faces great challenges!

What am I talking about? Today, the United States of America has a very, obsolete and inequitable Income Tax System and totally unacceptable levels of Drug Abuse; High School Drop Outs; Homeless; Hunger; Incarceration at Record Numbers; Low Wages; Mental Illness; Missing Children; Poverty; Teen Pregnancy; and Unemployment— Adult, Senior Adult Long Term and Teen. Most troubling of all is our almost twenty trillion dollars of National Debt which will literally destroy our Country, if US Government action to reduce the amount isn't taken soon!

Our Country pays more to lock up some men, women, and children than we pay to educate them. I truly wonder what God thinks about a Country that fails to feed, clothe, or educate its children properly. We waste millions of dollars in foreign countries whose citizens hate the United States of America: Hard earned tax dollars that could be better spent on Americans here at home!

We have too many politicians who get elected and re-elected through the power of lobby money. Once in Congress, they pay themselves extremely well with Dollars and Perks, never to return home, suffering from "Potomac Fever." We have Political Families, too, who mistakenly think that only they have the Presidential Leadership Skills necessary to lead this Country. Many of our leaders are willing to send other parent's children to perhaps die in Foreign Wars, but refuse to send their own. Defending one's Country while sometimes paying the ultimate sacrifice – Death on the Battlefield – is not a price many rich or political families are willing to pay today. The time has come for other Americans to step up to provide a new direction for this Nation.

AMERICAN CITIZEN SERVICE:

We should have a Mandatory two - year "AMERICAN CITIZEN SERVICE" Program. Immediately after High School Graduation, every new high school graduate must be **required** to participate. **No exceptions due to financial position, last name, or prior college admission**. Those young citizens who choose to serve two years in the US Military will be rewarded with current military pay and, once service is completed, a GI Bill that includes college or trade school tuition plus full VA benefits.

Others who desire to serve in a Civic Position will receive room, board, a small monthly salary plus a college or trade school tuition program, following completion of the two years of "American Citizen Service." These Civic Positions can be created throughout America: In city, county and national parks, schools, nursing homes, hospitals both public and private, home repair, new home construction, and civil infrastructure. High School drop outs at any age may secure "Civic Positions", be provided the opportunity to earn a GED, and be employed in their Community: A young life helped is a young life saved.

These programs can be funded with monies saved by keeping America's Military nose out of other Countries problems that do not threaten our national security. We have tried that approach for fifty years. Look at the success we have achieved with such a U.S. Government policy to date: **Almost twenty trillion dollars in National debt.** The US Military can run these programs as was done with the Civilian Conservation Core and the Works Progress Administration under the Franklin Delano Roosevelt Administration during the 1930's. My Uncles all told me the "C.C.C.'s & W.P.A." were Life Savers for many men and their families, especially ours.

Our Country will be better for it when all young citizens participate in a program to serve their fellow citizens. I cannot tell you how many men in their fifties and sixties tell me today they wish they had served their country in the military when they were younger. I always say I probably would not have served had I not been forced by The Universal Military Draft. The experiences of those days are unforgettable and the memories are priceless. I still get Christmas cards from men who served with me in my US Army Basic Training Platoon. For those boys and girls who think their brains and future are too valuable to be invested in public or military service, I would point out just **SOME** of the many famous Celebrities and Athletes who served Uncle Sam prior to their success in civilian life:

US ARMY = Celebrities

Claude Akins, James Arness, Neville Brand, Mel Brooks, Art Carney, Ossie Davis, Charles During, Robert Duvall, Jimmy Hendrix, William Holden, George Kennedy, Kris Kristofferson, Burt Lancaster, Audie Murphy, Elvis Presley, Dale Robertson, Mickey Rooney, Kurt Vonnegut, Efren Zimbalist, Jr.

US ARMY = Athletes

Rock Bleir, Joe DiMaggio, Bob Kalsu, Joe Lewis, Rocky Marciano, Willy Mays, Jackie Robinson, Pat Tillman.

US AIR FORCE = Celebrities

Gene Autry, Charles Bronson, Johnny Cash, William Conrad, Clark Gable, Charlton Heston, Walter Matthau, Jack Palance, Jimmy Stewart.

US AIR FORCE = Athletes
Tom Landry, Archie Williams.
US MARINES = Celebrities
Don Adams, Bea Arthur, Glen Ford, Sterling Hayden, Brian Keith, Lee Marvin, Ed McMahon, Steve McQueen, Tyrone Power, John Russell, George C. Scott, Jonathan Winters.
US MARINES = Athletes
Patty Berg, Jerry Coleman, Ken Norton, Leon Spinks, Lee Trevino, Ted Williams.
US NAVY = Celebrities
Eddie Albert, Richard Boone, Humphrey Bogart, Ernest Borgnine, Johnny Carson, Bill Cosby, Sammy Davis Jr., Kirk Douglas, Henry Fonda, Jack Lemmon, Paul Newman, Jason Robards, Robert Stack, Rod Stieger.
US NAVY = Athletes
Yogi Berra, Bob Feller, David Robinson, Roger Staubach, Jesse Ventura, John Wooden.
US COAST GUARD = Celebrities
Dennis Hopper, Cesar Romero.

I also feel that many young people in the inner city would have a better life through such an organized program of personal development. I went through US Army Paratrooper School at Fort Benning, Georgia, leading a platoon of young men: three nineteen—year - old boys in particular who were from South Chicago, Illinois are most memorable. They were all over six feet tall and their average weight was 185 pounds. It was an education for those handsome and very virile young men to meet a twenty-five-year-old logger from Washington State (I stood five feet four inches tall and was a very well built 150 pound man.) who could teach with fairness and resolve even those outstanding physical and mental specimens a few lessons of manly conduct. With the guidance and leadership of a very rugged and unforgettable Black American Sergeant Major, I must quickly add!! (I had to laugh when "Top" said the only thing these boys needed really was their Grandmother around to take a switch to their rear ends ever so often!)

When the challenge was completed, I told the three fellows how pleased I was with their conduct after our "Discussion." I also told them how much I envied their God Given Talent, Good Looks, and Future. I have often wondered what successful careers and outstanding lives these men have enjoyed; certainly they each had a great opportunity in Uncle Sam's Army. I pray they made the most of it. Undoubtedly, these three men would have made very successful Top Sergeants or Commissioned Officers, if a career in the Military was desired. These impressive fellows absolutely possessed the courage, intelligence and physical characteristics required for success in the US Army. With proper training and encouragement, these brave paratroopers would soon learn leadership by example, knowledge based upon experience and courage through confidence, honor, and Faith. I just pray our Country did not lose any of these three talented Soldiers in the horrible Viet Nam war.

I was drafted during a time called The "Berlin Crisis." While I was on active duty, I experienced the "Cuban Crisis" as a Private. (God loved us, because we were many.) I served in the 8ᵗʰ Data Processing Company at Fort Monroe, Virginia, a historic post on the James River. I drove a "Deuce and a Half" truck and made myself as humorously obnoxious, yet somewhat useful as possible! I wasn't doing what I truly wanted to be doing, but I quickly learned that a Private doesn't tell Uncle Sam what he's going to do. Uncle Sam gives the orders! Those Computer folks were some of the smartest people I have ever known; what a great bunch of outstanding Soldiers from all over the United States! It was a privilege to serve with them.

Fort Monroe, which at the time was Continental US Army Command Headquarters, was known in the United States Army as the "Little Pentagon"; Privates called this duty station the "Land of Sleeping Colonels." Moated Fort Monroe was a historic Post built of brick and stone at Hampton Roads, Virginia in the James River, overlooking Chesapeake Bay. Construction begin in 1819 and finished in 1844; it was an element of the Third System of Coastal Defenses in the aftermath of the War Of 1812. It was the only Federal installation in the upper South to remain in United States control throughout the Civil War. Early in their careers, Confederate Generals Joe Johnson and Robert E. Lee were stationed there; during the Civil War, President Abraham Lincoln met with General George B. McClellan at Fort Monroe after General McClellan's Peninsula Campaign;

after the Civil War, Confederate President Jefferson Davis was imprisoned there. It was a remarkable experience to serve as an Enlisted Soldier at a Historic Post of such a high level of Leadership: The Four Star Commanding General was John Waters, General George Patton's son-in-law. The second-in-command was Three Star Lieutenant General Louis Truman, President Harry Truman's nephew.

After active duty, I became a member of a United States Army Reserve 17th Special Forces "A" Team where I served for two years, prior to being honorably discharged. My "A" Team Commander was Major Mike Layton, a political writer for the Seattle Post Intelligencer. Originally from Wyoming, Major Layton served in World War II at the "Battle of the Bulge" when he was just eighteen years old. He was one of the finest Soldiers and Individuals that I have ever been privileged to know! Major Layton's common sense intellect and rock solid integrity were among the highest character traits I have ever personally witnessed in a fellow human being! When the Major gave an order, a soldier knew it was a wisely determined order of importance. I am very proud of having served in my Country's Military even though it was in a very small role of little importance. I assure you that I would always return to active duty at a moment's notice, if our nation's security were threatened; most Veterans I am certain feel the same way.

While an "American Citizen Service" program will cost money, I must point out the huge cost taxpayers may be facing to pay off bad guaranteed student loans. One must also consider the cost of the time that students have invested in college or trade school while failing to graduate. Plus, losing thousands of young people who grow up without proper parental guidance in poverty and unable to secure a sound Elementary, Middle and High School Education is unforgivable. Our Country is better than such treatment: The high costs that our society pays for adolescent drug use, illegitimate children, gang violence, and incarceration are costs which are totally unnecessary and shameful. How will the Country pay for a Universal Citizen Service Program? **ONE**: Stop throwing away hard-earned tax dollars on foreigners who hate Americans and all that we stand for. **TWO**: Stop encouraging high school graduates to attend college or trade school before they are ready financially or mentally. **THREE:** Stop the horrible cost to society of high school drop-outs.

AMERICAN GUARANTEED STUDENT LOAN DEBT:

Guaranteed Student Loan Catastrophe: Some say this is the next big financial bubble to face American taxpayers. Many American families face this crisis. Many students were persuaded by academic and student peer pressure to go directly to a four year college before they were ready mentally, or financially. Consequently, failure was pre-ordained.

We must either allow students to discharge their Student Loan debt through routine bankruptcy laws or via a Citizen's Service Program, similar to what some Physicians, Dentists or

Teachers do now. For the Federal Government to make money by earning interest on Student Debt is ridiculous, especially when our Country throws away billions of dollars on other Countries — many of whose citizens despise America.

In every way possible, The United States should be encouraging young people to secure a College or Trade School Education. Interest free student loans sound perfect to me. If we can make billionaires who make bad investment decisions financially whole, (Think Solyndra - - Alternative Energy to the tune of five hundred million dollars.) then our Country can afford to eliminate most, if not all, student loan debt interest.

Aspects of the Student Loan Debt problem which anger me are recruitment activities of some *For Profit Schools* who recruit naive or desperate job seeking students based totally upon false promises of high graduation rates as well as inflated post graduation employment rates. These shameful *For Profit Schools* have unfortunately been allowed to operate while being financed almost entirely by the Federal Student Loan Program.

During the 1980's, I represented what was considered by many in the Aviation Industry to be one of the finest aviation technical schools in the Country. The Tulsa, Oklahoma school was then part of an Orange County, California For Profit School empire. The executives of the operating company were extremely well paid and many became millionaires through Wall Street sales of company stock whose value was based upon Company profits. Gross Income totally depended upon successful nationwide recruitment of students who mostly depended upon either the Federal Student Loan Program or The Veterans Administration Education Program to pay high tuition fees. (Foremost among important recruitment selling tools were the high Union salaries earned by Airline Pilots and Mechanics at that time.)

*School student recruiters like myself, however, enjoyed less financial support. Sales territory operational expenses were entirely the responsibility of the Salesman: All travel expenses to visit with potential students or to give recruiting talks at High Schools were the total responsibility of the Sales Representative. The cost of motel rooms, meals and any other expenses were never reimbursed. Believe it or not, the school expected all recruitment costs to be covered by a Sales Representative collecting a $100.00 "Application Fee" from a Family, following a Student interview (Sales Presentation). I can't count the number of times I heard the school recruiting sales manager say: "What are you talking about, Nelson? What do you mean you can't get a hundred dollars from the kid or his parents! Are you kidding me, (you idiot)? You're forgetting 'Grandma's Cookie Jar'! Every Grandma always has a hundred dollars hidden away in her 'Cookie Jar', just for Johnny's use for school. You need to **Get (steal) That Money, Nelson**!"*

Frankly, I always felt like a common thief in taking such money from any Family. Many times I suspected the hundred dollars was badly needed for food or bills. Unfortunately, no other money was forthcoming from the company unless and until a student actually showed up in Tulsa to enroll in school. In my sales territory of Washington, Oregon, Idaho and Alaska, recruiting High School Students was very difficult due to the geographical location of the school, school tuition, cost of living, part time job availability in Tulsa, and even the Family's doubt about the wisdom of such a career or school choice. I, however, was thrilled to be encouraging young people to consider a career in the field of Aviation. I am afraid it was a fact of life: I loved Aviation so much that, regrettably, I made a poor employer choice. After a year, I did leave the company. Much to my delight, one of my Recruits is now a top Check Pilot for Alaskan Airlines! A few others are Professional Aviation Mechanics.

The Federal Government should never allow *For Profit Schools* to operate student recruitment sales territories without the school providing a living income with health benefits for its sales people, if the school wishes to utilize the Federal Student Loan Program. Also, and more importantly, *For Profit Schools* should not be allowed to receive one dime of Federal Student Loan money until a student completes his education or chooses to leave school with funds apportioned on the basis of courses actually taken. *For Profit Schools* are businesses: Require *For Profit Schools* to use other financial sources for operating money; stop allowing schools to operate by, in effect , "Stealing" Federal Student Loan money from vulnerable students, many of whom fail to complete their studies due to overall financial problems primarily, I suspect.

On Line Education Programs are an entirely different matter: Not one dime of Federal Student Loan money should be paid to an *On Line Education School* unless and until a student confirms to Government authorities that the school has satisfied his educational needs; and the school must certify that School Courses are properly accredited by an acknowledged professional educational organization, transferable to another school or a different school program.

Anyone involved in Federal Student Loan Fraud should be sentenced to a non – probationary period of five years or more, if convicted in a Court of Law. Repayment of taxpayer's money by the thief must be required, even if it takes the thief's entire lifetime. Stealing from Taxpayers through the Federal Student Loan Program must STOP! Convicted thieves must fully repay the taxpayer!

Schools who prey on Military Veterans anger me the most. When Veterans put their lives on the line in Wars overseas, it is unconscionable to have their precious Veterans Administration Education Funds wasted (stolen) here at home: By unknowingly attending *On Line Schools* NOT accredited by Professional Organizations; by taking courses or earning degrees of little vocational or educational value, as determined by Industry Professionals; by receiving course credits that are not transferable to other schools, when requested by the student; and, ultimately, by schools that promise Veterans Living Income employment opportunities upon graduation, but deliver either no job at all or one with inadequate compensation.

Finally, *For Profit Schools* who promote educational degrees which Industry Employers will not accept as indicative of competency in a particular field should not be allowed by the Fair Trade Commission to advertise to recruit Students. For certain, these schools (crooks) should NEVER be allowed to utilize the Federal Student Loan Program.

AMERICAN INCOME TAXES:

We must stop the destruction of the Middle Class that drives our economic engine: We must replace free trade with fair trade that will put Americans back to work so Americans can earn a living wage income with health benefits to start paying income taxes. If other countries place tariffs on our exports, we must retaliate with tariffs on their products. It is high time to think of America FIRST and put our people back to work! We must change the tax code that over time has allowed 20 percent of the people to own over 89 percent of the privately held wealth in the United States. Use the US Justice System to attack and close foreign tax shelters and havens. There must be a heavy penalty for corporations hiding excessive retained earnings off shore, as determined by Professional Accountants. Non – probationary jail time for offending executives sounds perfect.

There should be absolutely no doubt about where I stand on corporate taxes — I believe in moving toward a 10 percent corporate income tax as soon as possible. (But not until our national debt has been significantly reduced or eliminated!) Corporations do not pay taxes — customers do. A well-managed corporation is a very efficient method of running a business enterprise. A 10 percent corporate income tax rate would make the United States very competitive in foreign trade.

Perhaps The United States should consider a **Fair Tax** charged against ALL income, municipal bond interest and capital gains as well as earned income, with the elimination of all loopholes or deductions. (Add just one deduction and before you know it, because of the power of lobby groups, you have once again added them all.) **Perhaps we should consider a special tax with a sunset clause just paid by the aforementioned wealthy top 20 percent to help pay off the national debt. Perhaps most Ultra-Wealthy Americans Would Be Willing To Participate If They Were Guaranteed Through Legislation That The Money Would Go To Just Reducing The National Debt.** Wise men and women who are experts in the field of Economics, Budgets, and Taxes need to be consulted AND FOLLOWED!

AMERICAN INDIAN:

Too often the American Indian has suffered in lonely rural isolation and on the mean streets of our large cities. America should always do what it can financially, socially, and politically to help its American Indian Citizens. The federal government must strive to create social, economic, and medical programs to better American Indian lives. Some Native American Indians groups have the highest rate of diabetes in the world. Thank God for American Indian gambling casinos which are an economic godsend for many Tribes.

Recently, I saw a TV interview with an American Indian Author who was foolishly criticizing the fact that US Army Buffalo Soldiers of the 9th and 10th Cavalry were awarded Congressional Medals of Honor, while fighting his Fore Fathers. Let me remind the Author that his people were some of the most ferocious Warriors the American Military has ever faced anywhere in the world. Those Indians were fighting for their people, land and way of life; unfortunately, the tribes were fighting against the unstoppable Western Expansion of the United States of America. (Bows and arrows against carbines and cannon ! The end result was guaranteed.) If a Buffalo Soldier was the recipient of the Congressional Medal of Honor, believe me dear Author, the man earned it. Furthermore, I believe the 19 Black Buffalo Soldiers and 4 Seminole Indian Scouts, who were the recipients of the Congressional Medal of Honor during the days of the Western Frontier, should all be honored by being laid to rest at Arlington National Cemetery with the rest of America's War and National Heroes. (Nine are already there.) Buffalo Soldiers helped make the West safe for settlement. These men put their lives on the line for their fellow Americans; some of whom paid the ultimate sacrifice— Death On The Battlefield.

Finally, I pray that by the time this book is published the Multi-Billionaire owner of the National Football League Washington, D.C. Team has used common sense to change his team's name. The proud American Indian has been insulted enough by society. I wonder how quickly and with what ferocious indignation American Black people (who dominate the player's roster in the NFL) would react if the name of the team was the Washington Blacks, or something worse. I just will never understand why we in the United States have to go through life mistreating or insulting others because of the color of one's skin. If the NFL doesn't attack this despicable problem with the aggressiveness of a Seattle Seahawk Linebacker, Congress and the President should. U.S. Citizens should never forget that Collegiate Football All-American Mr. Jim Thorpe (Carlisle Indian Industrial School), a Sac and Fox American Indian from Oklahoma who was named the greatest athlete of the twentieth century, played professional football for seven teams over 15 years, and helped establish the professional game. Furthermore, Mr. Jim Thorpe became the first President of the American Professional Football Association, which became the National Football League. Without question, Mr. Jim Thorpe and his Relatives need to be treated with greater respect and dignity. The NFL should be ashamed of itself for not stopping this humiliation immediately, once objections surfaced. The skin color of American Indians is given to them by the Great Spirit; Indian Tribes are offended by the current Washington NFL Team name. In the name of common sense and human dignity, change the name, please!

AMERICAN MILITARY:

(1) We must stop costly wars fought almost entirely by our Nation's poor and middle-class sons and daughters: If Universal Military Service were reinstated to allow the drafting of the sons and daughters of America's wealthy and elite citizens, I doubt if the United States would ever again go to war unless our country were threatened with extinction. If ever we do go to war again, we should only fight wars of total annihilation, like the United States fought World War II. When we fight, we must fight with a deadly determination to win! Our government officials must stop wasting money in foreign countries trying to make (buy) friends of people who hate us. Let's stay home and mind our own business. Let's keep our powder dry and our Troops safe, unless and until the United States of America is truly threatened with extinction.

(2) It is the Department of DEFENSE, Not OFFENSE: Do not misunderstand me: I always want our Country to be the most powerful Military Power in the World. We must fund the Department of Defense with whatever money sound financial management dictates and our current budget allows. I just see no need to waste tax dollars and beautiful American lives fighting other countries' wars. **I Repeat: It is the Department of DEFENSE, Not OFFENSE.** Once a Secretary of State of the United States asked, "What good is a Military if we cannot use it?" The answer must always be: "Our Great Military must NEVER be used foolishly in wars that are none of our business and in which our national security is not at stake." By the way, I encourage the Former Secretary to pick up a weapon, get off what the Airborne calls HER fourth point of contact, and put HER life on the line, instead of needlessly and very foolishly placing the lives of OUR children at risk.

(3) The United States must provide whatever Health Care and Disability Resources are required to take care of all our VETERANS — now and for as long as necessary: The United States Department of Veterans Affairs must always be funded adequately. Our military heroes who fought our foreign wars should not be forced to fight for health care and disability payments here at home.

(4) Military Desegregation: All Americans should thank God for the Post World War II US Military and President Harry S. Truman. In 1948, Mr. Truman wanted to get re-elected: He needed the Black vote, pure and simple. (sound familiar?) At the same time, he wanted to initiate Universal Military Training; however, Black Civil Rights Leaders did not want young Black men serving in a segregated Military. Thus on July 26, 1948, President Harry S. Truman signed and issued Executive Order 9981 which ordered "equality of treatment for all persons in the armed services without regard to race, color, religion or national origin."

Initially, as in any bureaucracy (especially the Military), it took a while to fully implement the Desegregation Order. The United States Air Force under the direction of Secretary Stuart Symington moved to desegregate quickly; The US Navy, too, but slower; The US Army, however, initially resisted. But, Fate does work sometimes in unique ways: Because of a combat loss of White Troops during the Korean War, Black Troop replacements were quickly integrated into the US Army. By October 1953, the US Army announced that 95 percent of African-American Soldiers were serving in integrated units.

There were no Black families living in my home town: The Brown Family described in "Rock Hill" was pure fiction to give the author the opportunity to write about the amazing World War II Aerial Accomplishments of the Tuskegee Airman and the segregation I witnessed in the South in 1962 and 1963. In 1957, I met my first Black people at the University of Washington in the dorm, the classroom and on the University of Washington Husky Freshman Football practice field: I was awed by their brains, brawn and overall kindness to me. (Don't get me wrong: If there was a 38th team, I was on the 39th! In truth, I wasn't much of a competitive threat to my fellow Teammates who later won two Rose Bowl Games, after I was long gone!)

I was drafted into the US Army in October 1961; then transferred to the South in 1962. That time was an unforgettable period in my life. I arrived in the State of Virginia after flying "Call Me Lucky" from Fort Lewis, (Tacoma), Washington to Williamsburg, Virginia by "Pilotage" (Looking out the window of the plane). The flight was a genuine opportunity for me to learn that America is a beautiful, huge Country with wonderful people everywhere; the flight was very challenging and most memorable, especially dancing with a blue eyed blonde one night in Dodge City, Kansas! Funny how the beautiful memory of young "Conspicuous Attractiveness" lasts forever, though time has indeed flown away!

In the US Army, I was given a solid education why one should not judge another just by the color of skin. However, seeing the signs that stated, "Whites Only" / "Colored Only" bathrooms and drinking fountains off post Fort Monroe, Virginia was a culture shock which made no sense to me or anyone else in our Unit. Most Soldiers in our 8th Data Processing Unit were from the West Coast like me; all were astonished at the segregation we observed.

During my four years in the US Army (two Active, two Reserve), many Black Commissioned and Non Commissioned Officers were extremely helpful in providing my Military Leadership and Personal Development. I consider myself very fortunate to have served under these very Professional Soldiers, most of whom were World War II and Korean War Veterans who had yet to serve 20 years of Active Duty prior to Retirement. These Professional Soldiers were true War Heroes who had fought and defeated the Germans, Japanese and North Koreans. My Immediate Supervisor was a White Top Sergeant from the State of Oklahoma, a decorated Combat Veteran who fought in Europe, Korea and Viet Nam. I was honored just to have known Sergeant Leroy Simmons, let alone to have served under his very Professional Command.

Thank God, President Truman issued Executive Order 9981. Likewise, thanks to the outstanding US Navy, US Army and US Air Force Generals and Admirals who carried out the order successfully. Today, the US Military is undoubtedly all the better for it. By the way, I must especially congratulate the Generals of the US Marines for their efforts in desegregating the Corps. The US Marines will always be very special to me. *I had the privilege of attending US Army Paratrooper School at Fort Benning, Georgia with a US Marine Pathfinder Team. I have thought of those outstanding men often. The US Marine Sergeant in charge of the Pathfinder Team said to me: "You should have been a Marine, Nelson." Plus, my Valley City, North Dakota State Teachers College Football Coach, Mr. Vernon Gale (All Skyline Conference First Team as a Single Wing Fullback at the University of Wyoming), was a Marine. (I idolized this magnificent example of a Man's Man.) He, too, said, "Join the Marines, Nelson. They will challenge a guy like you!" Also, on the Valley City Viking Team were three outstanding Athletes and Scholars who had served in the US Marines prior to attending State Teachers College - - Mr. Ron Estes; Mr. Bill Svenkesen and Mr. Mike Vanyo. We have remained friends for over fifty years based upon my genuine respect and admiration for these three very accomplished men. I must sincerely thank them for overlooking my sense of humor and other rather obvious faults! But, the Universal Military Draft came along when I was "setting chockers around logs" while working for my Dad during the week day and busy practicing my "moves" on a tavern dance floor on Friday and Saturday nights. (much to the dismay of my Mom, I must add!) Not a "Jar Head" but a proud "Dog Face", I shall always be!*

Just the same, all Americans shall always owe a debt of thanks to the US Military for how well they have led the

way in ending **Racial Discrimination in the United States. Implementing President Truman's Executive Order 9981 wasn't easy; but it was necessary. Desegregation has certainly made us a better Military, Country and People.**

(5) Military Cyber War: It is said that intellectual property theft costs the United States 300 billion dollars a year and 1.2 million jobs. Cyber-espionage directed at the United States is considered by some to be the greatest transfer of wealth in human history: This must stop and The United States Military must be at the fore front of its elimination. If the culprits will not cease, then the "Nuclear Cyber Option" must be employed: Sever the internet connection between those countries and the United States. This may sound beyond the pale to some, but such action is better than the economic destruction of the United States.

(6) Military Drone Aircraft: Those who object to the use of Drone Aircraft to fight Terrorism should join the U.S. Army (regardless of age, sex, or religion), pick up a rifle and go to the tribal territories of Pakistan and fire away. Or better yet, send your children to die by the hands of people who hate the United States of America and all the freedoms we stand and fight for.

(7) Military Rules of Engagement: The ONLY American Military Rules of Engagement that should exist should be to use whatever firepower is necessary to totally annihilate our enemies, including the Atomic and Hydrogen Bomb, **if the United States is attacked first with such weapons. PERIOD !**

It is long past time to untie our Brave US Military Personnel's arms from behind their backs with stupid Gentlemen's Agreements to properly fight cowards who from miles away electronically blow up our Gallant Men and Women with IED's.

During World War II when we fought to win at all costs, innocent people died in combat, but the Allies defeated the Japanese and German Military thugs who killed far more of their own innocent people. We ended that horrible catastrophe relatively quickly. **Then, most of our men and women came home to loved ones with the War Definitely Won and Over!**

Superior Officers sitting at their desks out of harm's way should do everything possible to provide overwhelming military support when requested by Troops in the Field facing death. Superior Officers of whatever rank should be immediately drummed out of the Military when Brave American men and women die because of out right Command Stupidity. Give those foolish Officers a dishonorable discharge as Military Officers are quick to do to Enlisted Personnel who make serious, costly mistakes on the Battlefield.

Lest anyone think I am Anti-Officer, take that thought from your mind. I had a very bright, distinguished, high ranking and extremely competent Officer – A West Pointer - - tell me: "Nelson, there truly is **RHIP** *- - Rank Has Its Privilege; but at the same time, there is* **RHIR - -** *Rank has its Responsibilities. Good conscientious, competent Officers know the difference and practice* **Both at the appropriate time.***"*

(8) Military Service Academies: It is long past time to require all Military Service Academy Graduates to serve a minimum of 10 years of Active Duty immediately after graduation, not five - - not an excessive price to pay for a two hundred and fifty thousand dollar education with the additional opportunity for a career in the United States Military. I served with a few West Point Graduates. All were absolutely outstanding in their Character and Leadership. These very capable people should serve in some type of Civic Leadership Position, helping build our Communities the second five years. Change Laws, if need be. Or, transfer this National Treasure to State National Guard Units for utilization.

By the way, it is a good thing I am not Commandant of West Point: **First,** *I would require the Professors (Teachers) to start each week by reciting the "Private's Prayer" —*

"Dear God,

"Please give my Captain the courage to make timely and competent decisions; the wisdom to know the difference between right and wrong; and the perseverance to stay the course until the mission is successfully accomplished and a little good luck wouldn't hurt either! (Although a Warrior usually makes his own Good Luck, to paraphrase Five Star General Douglas MacArthur.) AMEN"

OR, better yet ,— the General's Order - - "Always take care of your Troops, Officers, and, in turn, your Troops will always take care of you."

Second, I would require every Cadet annually to stand in front of General Armstrong Custer's Grave Site in the West Point Cemetery to be reminded of what happens when a Foolish Officer's Pride and Presidential Ambition overwhelms Character and Common Sense. I prefer that no Officer commit Military Suicide through Command Stupidity, but if you are so inclined, please do not take your brave American Troops with you!

(9) Military Sexual Assault: This is a crime and must be addressed and stopped immediately. All military personnel deserve our respect and legal protection without question.

At a time when all military personnel face IED and other lethal threats on a terrorist battlefield, our fighting men and women should not have to worry about sexual assault by anyone, especially superior officers. Our Top Military Leaders should be ashamed of their failure to act immediately and appropriately as military and civilian law requires. "The Top Brass" are very Honorable Professionals; I know they will correct this problem quickly and with common sense. If I am in error, however, and "The Top Brass" does not act quickly and adequately to correct this problem, Congress and the President must act expeditiously to move the prosecution of this unforgivable crime outside the Military Chain of Command.

CHILD PROSITUTION:

Men and women who force children to work as prostitutes should be dealt with severely in the Criminal Justice

System. Law breakers convicted by a Jury of their peers should receive non-probationary minimum prison sentence of five years or more.

Child prostitution is a despicable crime against society as a whole and beautiful young minds and bodies in particular. Because most victims are the result of poverty, single parent homes, poor parental supervision or just a simple lack of love for the child, society must do more to intercede before families self-destruct. Those who take advantage of young children for financial gain through the sex trade are the most despicable of mankind. Their crimes are unforgivable. Criminals who prey on children should be treated harshly by society.

What adults do of their own volition is totally fine with me. Sex between two consenting adults is their affair, regardless of the act or sex of the two people. However, it is sad when some women have to sell their bodies because it is their only way to make a living. God gave most of us a sound mind to be developed; unfortunately, because of poverty or mis-treatment such as child prostitution, some are denied the opportunity for a proper education. Law enforcement nationwide should take a special interest to stop this destruction of our youth. Special education programs featuring quality homes with loving supervision should be provided to those children who need support. A child lost or thrown away by a society that does not care about ALL of its children is an affront to God and decent people everywhere. The Federal Bureau of Investigation and Law Enforcement Officials Nationwide should be praised for their continued vigilance in the child sex trade business.

CLIMATE CHANGE:

We must end the costly dispute over climate change. We have melting glaciers, increasing numbers of powerful hurricanes and tornadoes, drought, record snowfall, rain, heat, and wind. These events are all signs there is a definite problem; we must **DETERMINE THE FACTS**. If necessary, let's reduce our carbon footprint. Perhaps a "Manhattan Project" is needed, devoted to learning how to create "clean coal", if possible. Some of the highest-paying middle-class jobs for the working men and women of this country exist in the coal industry. Before we throw more hardworking Americans out of work, we should try to solve the carbon footprint problems of burning coal. However, global warming appears real and should no longer be ignored; the Country must act to do what is necessary to solve this problem.

DRUG WAR:

We have wasted a trillion dollars of taxpayer's money on an unwinnable Drug War: It is time to admit defeat —legalize it, control it, tax it, and educate Citizens on why it is best not to use it unwisely (whatever "It" is, to quote a former President who didn't inhale!). We must learn from the costly lessons of alcohol prohibition and listen to our *ENLIGHTENED* Police Professionals and Federal and States Attorneys General. My recommendation is to NEVER use recreational drugs, but if one does, do so in the privacy of one's own home and never, ever drive under the influence of alcohol or narcotics. Society should keep an open mind about cannabis, however. Stories I have been told by Health Professionals of the healing and pain reduction/elimination properties of cannabis are remarkable. Muscular dystrophy, cancer and epilepsy are just a few of the infirmities successfully treated to enable a sick or dying human being to endure painful human misery until God calls. The National Institutes of Health and Drug Industry Scientists should be allowed by law to fully investigate the amazing therapeutic potential of cannabis.

It is reported in the press we have now incarcerated over two million Americans, mostly for drug crimes. The Drug War has created a massive prison industry. At the same time, some law enforcement personnel have been turned into legal thieves by allowing police to confiscate and keep thousands of dollars of cash and personal items including automobiles, when an individual is charged with drug possession. Twenty-year mandatory prison sentences not subject to parole or a judge's discretion is a law long overdue for change: Such treatment by the Police and the Court System is a crime against human decency. Justice it is NOT.

With no legitimate means to make a living to provide for a family, some men and women will turn to illegality to survive. We must bring back the jobs to America that have been exported to foreign countries. With employment comes income; with living wage income comes the honorable means to feed and clothe a family. All Americans desire and deserve such an opportunity.

Experts say the horrible Drug War in Mexico, which has cost thousands of lives and millions of dollars, is caused by America's insatiable demand for what are now illegal recreational drugs. It is time now to help our neighbor to the South by legalizing recreational drugs in The United States. We must create legal channels of distribution and marketing. We must pass appropriate taxes on recreational drugs to generate revenue to run our Country and to help pay off our national debt.

The terrible scourge of heroin use by teenagers initiated by improper use of prescription drugs for pain or pleasure must be attacked through a Federal Program of intervention by Health Professionals. A Federal Good Samaritan Law to encourage drug overdose reporting to 911 operators without legal repercussion to callers must be passed. FDA must allow over the counter sale of the drug Naloxone which is used to counteract heroin overdose. Immediately, we must turn our drug war into a life saving campaign waged by all Americans led by Health Professionals. America is losing too many young people because of Government and Citizen inaction.

We must continually educate our citizens about the dangers of misuse of recreational drugs. Using recreational drugs foolishly is really no different than improperly using alcohol, cigarettes or prescription drugs: We must always use Education to tell our Children why it is best not to use recreational drugs. Continuing to make recreational drugs illegal, however, just creates an underground system where financial greed drives illicit activity.

EDUCATION:

We have a School Drop Out Crisis in this Country: Fortunately, America is making progress through Teacher evaluation tied to student performance, common core teaching standards and charter schools. However, when Teachers inflate student test scores to earn monetary bonuses, the integrity of the program is destroyed. Teachers, Administrators and State Officials must be encouraged to continue their quest to improve graduation rates. Those students not interested in a college or university education must have access to quality vocational training during or following High School. America will always need professional tradesmen and women to build our homes, solve our electrical and plumbing problems, and maintain our automobiles. A professional trade is an honorable career.

Wise and dedicated Teachers are the keys to our nation's future. The mental and physical development of our children is the single most important answer to most, if not all, of the future problems of the United States. How we educate our students will be indicative of our country's desire to improve the American way of life for all. The new push by our major corporations to emphasize STEM Programs (Science, Technology, Engineering and Mathematics) in America's

Middle and High schools are steps in the right direction to prepare our students to compete in the work place of the 21st Century. A Chief Executive Officer of one of our leading companies maintains America's ability to remain a leader in innovation is directly tied to our success in creating students who choose careers in Math and Science.

Critics of Common Core Teaching Standards always suggest they represent a "Dummying Down" of the educational system. It does not have to be! Set our education standards high throughout the United States to match the educational systems of States like Connecticut, Maryland and Massachusetts which rank at the top in our Country in educating children at all levels. Children in those States are truly no smarter than children in any other State. The key to Elementary, Middle and High School education is simple: Adequate funding for quality school facilities, Administrative Leaders and, above all, Teachers.

Here in the Bellevue Washington State School District, Administrators have just announced a new "Social and Emotional Learning Curriculum in grades 3 through 5 to help children work well together." It is called the "RULER": Recognizing, Understanding, Labeling, Expressing and Regulating emotion. Allegedly, this is a system which teaches skills to promote personal, social and work place success.

Wouldn't you know, this idea comes from one of the "Meccas" of Academia - - Yale University. It seems years of research shows that emotional literacy skills support academic success and promote "School Engagement," whatever that is. Apparently, students who "Recognize and Regulate their emotions are more focused on instruction and invested in learning." Emotional skills, the intelligentsia maintain, create a platform for "taking academic risks", whatever they are.

*I just wish the Bellevue School District would do a better job of teaching students: " RWAAH": **R**eading, **W**riting and **A**rithmetic from the first grade on; a solid foundation in **A**merican **H**istory would be a Godsend as well. Also, a few extra sessions of recess and more physical education programs would undoubtedly be great for young growing minds and bodies, too.*

Recently, I returned to my old home town: What a shock! Most of the timber has long been cut; little logging and lumbering employment remains. Most jobs are in the fields of Christmas Tree, Flower and Blueberry Farms: All are low or minimum wage employment opportunities.

Early in the morning, I went to my old High School to see the Senior Graduation pictures which were always hung in the old High School building hallways. To my surprise, the pictures were missing. As I walked from the what is now the Middle School Building, a gorgeous woman in her 40's stopped me and said, "May I help you, Sir?" I replied, "Yes, thank you, are you a Secretary or a Teacher?" She said, "Sir, (Which sounded like 'Dummy') I am the School Superintendent! Now, who are you and how may I help?" I told her I was a graduate of the Class of 1957 and I was looking for my Graduation Picture. She smiled and said, "All of the Graduation pictures are now hanging in the cafeteria in the High School Building. Come with me Mr. Nelson, I will take you there."

When we entered the cafeteria, there was a line of over 100 hundred children waiting for Breakfast, many Mexican American. The Superintendent saw my look of surprise. She said, "Yes, our Student Body has changed dramatically since you lived here, Jim." Working for less than a living wage is undoubtedly very prevalent in the Community now. The Real Estate Tax Base (adjusted for inflation since 1957) to support the school system has probably diminished considerably, too.

Later, as I drove around my old hometown, it looked quite different than what I remembered. There were abandoned homes and other buildings in dire need of fresh paint. It made me very sad to see a community, formerly a picture of economic vitality and once a very vibrant place in which to grow up, now changed by Father Time.

Employment featuring a living wage must be a Hallmark of all America, not just in certain areas of the fortunate. Likewise, a more equal distribution of Federal, State, County and Local taxes for education throughout a state must be initiated to provide a quality, equal education system for all children: City, Suburban and Rural, not just in the enclaves of the Wealthy. No School System left behind will insure that no child is left behind.

ELECTIONS;

Initiate Tax- Payer - Funded Elections with a Limit on Total Expenditures: Lobby groups, whether they be individuals, corporations, union, or non-profit, must be limited to a maximum amount of dollars each may spend in any election. Stop unlimited lobby spending NOW! Send lobbyists to jail for a minimum of five years for misusing the system. Good people have been voted out of office; others who perhaps should have been replaced were retained by the power of lobby money. The staggering amount of money involved in elections is a recent phenomenon. The dollars are mindboggling. Elected offices are now in large part bought and sold: SHAMEFUL! Citizens - United type activities are destroying this great nation. **If necessary, pass a law that specifically states that corporations ARE NOT citizens!** I pray change will come; however, I realize we cannot change the lobbying system easily due to fierce resistance by those who gain by such activities. Ultimately, the only answer may be a Constitutional Amendment.

END OF LIFE DECISIONS:

The huge expenditures that Medicare pays Hospitals and Physicians for Health Care at the end of the lives of some Seniors are outrageous. A Senior whose life is maintained **ONLY** when hooked up to Life Support Equipment (sometimes for months) is a terrible theft of taxpayer dollars.

I suspect in large part the fault lies with the Chief Decision Makers : **ONE**, Hospital Administrators who have a selfish desire to get every dollar that can be squeezed from the taxpayer through Medicare to operate hospitals and, **TWO,** Physicians who have not shown the professional courage to tell Families that a Senior Loved One is going to die relatively soon, regardless of what medical procedure is tried; that additional medical care will only prolong the inevitable pain and suffering of a Senior Loved One; and that it is time to save the taxpayer money by letting the Senior Loved One die in peace.

Americans of all ages must realize: We are born; we live for whatever time God gives and then we die. For Christians who profess it is a more blessed life in the Here After, I have never understood why some Christian Members of a Senior Loved One's Family do not admit that life has a beginning, a middle, and an end, which sometimes arrives sooner than some may wish. Unfortunately, there comes a time when the Senior Loved One must be allowed to go to God.

Medicare Data tells American Taxpayers that chronically ill patients in their last two years of life account for 27 to 30 per cent of Medicare spending. I have no doubt that millions of Medicare dollars can be saved by a more vigorous decision process in hospital rooms throughout America by "Just Saying NO" when Family members make foolish, costly and unreasonable requests to keep Senior Loved Ones alive, **only** through the use of Life Support Equipment. Yes, it may be done, but at what taxpayer cost? PLEASE LET ME BE CLEAR: If, however, there is scientific medical evidence that shows a Senior Loved One may "Pull Through", **Then YES, any and all medical procedures must be used.** But, if there is NO chance, Family members must then be encouraged (told) to allow their Senior Loved One to pass quietly to God, without unnecessary and costly delay.

*I am a prime example of what Medical Science is capable. I had a Cardiac Arrest. My life was saved in large part by, **FIRST**, immediate application of CPR by my US Army Chinook Helicopter Pilot Son who learned his skill in the Service of his Country; **SECOND,** the rapid professional response by the Bellevue Fire/Emergency Department Unit who worked quickly to stabilize my condition, prior to transporting me to Overlake Memorial Hospital in Bellevue, Washington; **AND THIRD,** upon arrival at Overlake Hospital, Medical Professionals took speedy action to give me aid and save my life. Thankfully, God and Professional Health Care smiled on me. I was placed into a medically induced coma. After forty eight hours, the Doctors slowly brought me out of the coma. As the hours passed, and I slowly began to respond, the Doctors informed my Family that my prognoses looked very good. All awaited my return to full consciousness. Everyone in the hospital room knew I was on my way to a complete recovery when I asked my Grandson, who was feeding me a sliver of an ice chip, "Can you spare it?" My Wife said everyone laughed and issued a sigh of relief, knowing that I still had my sense of humor!*

Quick Professional Emergency Response, Medical Science, Quality Health Care and many Prayers by my Family and

Friends saved this Old Salesman (Logger, Pilot, Football Linebacker, Husband, Father and Grandfather) from passing on to that Great Football Field, Sales Territory and Airport in the Sky to meet my God. For the loving lifesaving skill of my Son, the assistance of the Professionals, Medicare and the Mercy of my God, I give thanks. Whether the effort was worth it to my Family and others, remains to be seen. My wife claims I am still the same old opinionated, loud mouth as before the incident. I say it is my God given Constitutional Right, so there!

I do thank God as well for living in King County, Washington State: Our EMS / Medic One System has a Cardiac Arrest Survival Rate of 57 per cent of incidents; most of the Nation has only a Survival Rate of 10 percent, which is quite a difference! The average Medic Unit response time is a blessed 7.5 minutes. Considered to be one of the World's Best, our EMS / Medic One System is managed by the Emergency Medical Services Division Of Public Health for Seattle and King County; Dr. David Fleming is the Director and Top Health Officer; and the King County Executive is Mr. Dow Constantine. All Fire Departments, Paramedic Agencies, EMS Dispatch Centers and Hospitals in the System need to be praised for their outstanding Life Saving Record. Other areas of the world should copy the Seattle and King County EMS / Medic One System and perhaps enjoy similar Cardiac Arrest lifesaving success!

Once again, I do firmly believe that IF THERE IS A CHANCE, based solely upon medical evidence that recovery is possible, of course any and all Medical Science available must and should be used. However, if there is Absolutely NO CHANCE OR HOPE, then, a Senior Loved One must be allowed to Pass on to God with Dignity and Peace.

American taxpayers through Medicare paid over $50,000 for my medical and hospital bills. Was it worth it? Who knows? One thing that I do know for sure is that I have told my Family if anything similar happens to me in the future and I wind up on Life Support Equipment with no hope for recovery: "Please. Do not hesitate! Pull the Plug. Say Prayers in my behalf, be faithful, and let me pass on to a better home with God, saving the American Taxpayer precious funds at the same time." I have now initiated a Living Will and recommend one to others.

Citizens should know that official data shows: 27 to 30 percent of Medicare payments cover the cost of care for people in the last two years of life; and 12 percent of Medicare beneficiaries account for 70 percent of program spending, according to the Federal Health Care Financing Administration.

ENERGY;

We Need Energy Independence: We must expedite full use of our vast natural gas resources by building natural gas refueling stations across America and encouraging the timely switch to natural gas-burning trucks and automobiles.

Ground water contamination caused by the natural gas extraction "Fracking" process must be investigated and if indeed there are problems, they must be solved now. Our natural gas resources must be utilized for the economic and energy needs of America; it must, however, be done safely and judiciously.

ESTATE TAXES:

Estate Taxes must be raised to return the United States to a more equitable society. Having 20% of our population own 89% of our private wealth is unconscionable ! Lobbyists working in behalf of the wealthy have lowered Estate Taxes to enable the wealthy to pass on too much wealth to descendants. Perhaps a certain percentage of a much higher Estate Tax should be dedicated to reducing the horrible National Debt. Wealthy Citizens must remember that The United States is a Republic, not an Oligarchy.

Also, allowing the rich to escape Federal Estate Taxes by using State Law to create "Trusts in Perpetuity" is a terrible crime and must be stopped immediately: Federal Law trumps State Law. The ultra rich must share their great wealth with the Country upon their death. The United States economic system enabled the rich the means to create their enormous fortune; pay back time for their American Opportunities must occur when the rich buy their private jet ride to "God's Airport in the Sky."

By Lobbying (Paying Off) State Legislatures to legalize "Trusts in Perpetuity", the rich are able to avoid paying their fair share of Estate Taxes. And at the same time, descendents still own (in effect) and control their businesses, homes, and other valuable assets. "Perpetuity Trusts" even allow beneficiaries to avoid payment to creditors for personal debt or being sued for causing accidents or injuries, believe it or not! This theft of billions of dollars of Estate Tax dollars from the US Treasury must be stopped. New Estate Tax Laws must be passed and those who break the Law must be jailed and fined severely!

FARMERS:

Thank God for America's Farmers and their food. The greatest tools for peace the United States has are our World Food Programs. I believe in helping the Family Farmer in every way this Country can; I do not, however, believe in paying absentee owners who own Farms for tax write offs or as investment properties that are designed to profit not from farming, but totally from Government Support Programs.

God has blessed the United States of America with our hardworking Farmers and their abundant crops that feed the people of the United States and the World; all should thank God for HIS largess and our American Farmers who grow this Wondrous Bounty Of Food.

FOSTER CHIDREN:

Some Foster Child Programs are an Abomination: Just ask some adults who grew up in foster homes. President George W. Bush had the right idea with his Faith-Based Initiative Program; it was a step in the right direction. Group Homes sponsored by Religious Groups such as the Boles Children's Home in Texas of the Arms of Hope Organization (A Christian Environment Leading to Productive Citizenship) and Father Flannigan's Boys Town in Nebraska (Instills Boys Town Values to Strengthen Body, Mind and Spirit) are two great examples. Keeping brothers and sisters together in an atmosphere of love, respect and a faith based philosophy is a much better idea than some Foster Homes operated primarily to make money.

"Where Children have a Hope because Christians have a Heart."

—-Superintendant Gayle Oler (1943 – 1969) Boles Children's Home.

"The work will continue, you see, whether I am there or not, because it is God's work, not mine."—-Father Flannigan, Boys Town.

GAY RIGHTS:

We must give Gay men and Lesbian women equal rights as required by simple human decency: Who someone marries in this country is no one's business but the two individuals'. The arguments some religious Leaders use to fight against

Gay and Lesbian Right to Marriage is the same type of arguments Southerners used to argue **FOR SLAVERY: States Rights!** If I remember correctly, we fought a Civil War with over 600,000 men and women killed on the Battlefield to free the Slaves. It is time now, without bloodshed, to free American Gay and Lesbian Citizens to marry who they wish! Organized religion should be concerned with the here-after, not the here and now when their ugly interference concerns a basic American legal right.

GERRYMANDERING, IMMIGRATION AND THE VOTE:

We must stop the Gerrymandering of US House Districts which distorts true Political Will: This activity is Party Politics in its most evil form. We must fix the Immigration system with borders that are definitely closed to unlawful entry; we must allow those illegally here now a legal pathway to Citizenship in the United States with the right to register to vote. We simply must make it easier for all US Citizens to vote, regardless of race, creed or color; mean political party politics should not be allowed to hinder any Citizen's Constitutional Right To Vote. The Civil War has been over for almost 150 years; the North won! Some people, obviously, have yet to accept that fact. **Eventually, freeing the slaves gave those horribly mistreated people US Citizenship with the Constitutional Right to register to vote!**

GUNS: (WEAPONS) AND THE MENTALLY ILL:

The Second Amendment is the Law of the Land: We can pass a law to ban weapons of any kind; to totally eliminate them is another matter. The same is true of magazine clips. We must, however, confiscate and destroy weapons that are used to commit a crime. Arrest and prosecute those who commit crimes using weapons; and sentence those convicted to a minimum non-probationary period of five years. Initiate stricter background checks to attempt to deny felons and the mentally ill from access to lethal weapons. We must accept there are still no guarantees — no matter what we do. If there truly is a matter that should be settled on the state level, perhaps it is gun control. Most citizens in Montana and Wyoming think very differently about firearms than most citizens in New York and New Jersey, I suspect. Everyone should agree on the obvious: A weapon of any type should never be used for an illegal purpose; there should be a harsh consequence in a court of law for the user of that gun, if it is.

"Stand Your Ground Law" is a legal issue that should be settled at the Federal level. However, self defense is an established and accepted feature of our legal system; "Stand Your Ground Law", as passed today by some States, may be totally unnecessary. Legal and Judicial Authorities should be consulted and followed.

Frankly, I would rather keep track of a sick person who is suffering from a severe mental illness who may try to buy a weapon than a sane person who owns a weapon. At the same time, the Federal Government must fund and create the finest mental health program in the world with special hospitals / homes for those in need. Years ago when our society closed horrible insane asylums, our only answer at the time was to throw mentally ill people out in the street without either support or supervision, for heaven's sake! For those who suffer mental illness, lack of access to services and professional help must be corrected.

As reported in the Seattle Times, the State Of Washington is using our Prisons to house some of the mentally ill. We now have something called "Intensive Management Units" - - Classrooms within solitary confinement units where oversize school desks are bolted to the floor. Twice a week mentally ill offenders are let out of solitary confinement for cognitive behavior therapy classes. Prisoners (the mentally ill) are shackled to the desk during a group therapy lesson.

Dr Bruce Gage, the Washington State Department of Corrections' Chief Psychiatrist, estimates between 20 to 30 percent of Washington 16,700 inmates are mentally ill. "It used to be called 'De-Institutionalization'. Now it is called 'Trans-Institutionalization'. We (Society) took everyone out of the State Hospitals and the same population pretty much ended up in prisons and jails."

In 1955 before 'De-Institutionalization', there was one psychiatrist bed for every 300 US residents. Almost 50 years later, that ratio is 1 in 3,000. For every one person in a public or private psychiatric bed in Washington State, there are 3 people with a serious mental illness in the State's jails or prisons. America can and must do more for the mentally ill

HEALTH CARE;

We have a costly and Inadequate Healthcare System:
Perhaps the Affordable Care Act will solve our problems. Nothing works perfectly in the beginning. We must change the Affordable Care Act to make it better, if need be. To control costs, we have to know what the true costs are. We must request transparency in the healthcare system. If we attack the problems of obesity in this country through programs of exercise and better nutrition, perhaps healthcare costs would be significantly reduced. When people are in better shape physically and eat more wholesome food, they generally are in better health.

Hospital advertising should be banned by the Government, or at least greatly reduced. Today hospital industry advertising expenditures are almost three billion dollars. Some say one third of this sum is totally wasted by advertising worthless hospital rating systems or competitive medical procedure information. At the same time, television prescription drug advertising should be halted. I am sure research would show little is actually gained in consumer knowledge through such ads: Patient confusion might be a better description. Higher prescription drug prices are the only true result, I suspect.

I remember in the early 1970's I told a drug industry advertising agency house guest that I had no doubt the drug industry would advertise prescription drugs on television, if it were permitted by the FDA. The man got a very surprised look on his face and exclaimed "No Way. Never!" I know now the drug industry was planning such a move even then.

He was just surprised that "Hicks out in the Countryside" could suspect such a thing. The first and foremost dispenser of prescription drug information should always be Health Professionals. If the FDA does not take action to stop this costly nonsense, Congress and the President should! Television prescription drug advertising is now banned in many other major Countries of the World.

Medicare should stop paying over a thousand dollars for an electric scooter that most Seniors use when they do not FEEL like walking and otherwise treat as a toy. Many of these Seniors would be much better off if they forced themselves to walk more and ride less. With a Physician's prescription, Medicare should allow a payment of two hundred dollars for a ReboundAir. This remarkable piece of cellular exercise equipment is 68 percent more efficient than a treadmill (as proven by NASA-sponsored research) and is the only piece of exercise equipment that will build bone. Anyone can read the remarkable story of ReboundAir and the world's most foremost authority on rebound exercise, Mr. Albert E. Carter, at www.ReboundAir.com. Mr. Bob Hope used the ReboundAir daily until his passing at the age of ninety-nine. Even President Ronald Reagan used a ReboundAir upstairs in the White House to maintain his physical fitness. I encourage all to rebound throughout life, as I do once a day for 15 minutes; you will be in better health if you do. By the way, if you wish to buy the world's finest manufactured ReboundAir you can order on—line or call: 1-888-464-5867. Just mention my name (Jim - Buddy

Nelson). Commission from the sale of the ReboundAir in my name will be used to provide a free ReboundAir to Senior Centers around the USA. (I am always amused when one sees the word "Free" today. Unfortunately, there is nothing "Free" — someone always has to pay! All too often, it is the taxpayer. That is fine, too, as long as "Free" does not mean "Wasted".)

Another inexpensive, fantastic wellness product is the Clark Enterprises Elite Passive Exerciser. This remarkable piece of passive exercise equipment has proven itself to provide pain relief for Seniors (and Americans of all ages) who suffer back problems, fibromyalgia, poor circulation and arthritis. The Elite Passive Exerciser has even been successfully used by Seniors in wheel chairs to reduce edema in the ankles. As part of my daily exercise routine, I have used a Clark Enterprises Elite Passive Exerciser for almost five years now. Because of my very active young life, I occasionally suffer from lower back pain. Twenty minutes on the Elite Passive Exerciser helps reduce the pain. I plan to use this machine until I pass.

The cost of the Elite Passive Exerciser machine is less than four hundred dollars — approximately what a few trips to a Chiropractor or a Medical Doctor would cost. Both Medicare and Medicaid should allow payment for this outstanding piece of passive exercise equipment. Go On Line to order at www.cwmachines.com or call 1-800-748-7172. Tell them Jim or Buddy Nelson sent you. The commission from your purchase of the Elite Passive

Exerciser, if my name is used, will be paid to provide a free machine for a Senior Center somewhere in the United States.

Many physicians, nurses, physical therapists, chiropractors and other Health Professionals have recommended the use of the Elite Passive Exerciser for the relief of pain; patient testimonials are truly significant.

HOMELESS IN AMERICA:

Churches around the United States should take note of what Plymouth Congregational Church in Seattle, Washington is doing to help solve our Nations Horrible, Homeless Crisis.

The Plymouth Housing Group, a Non-Profit founded by the Plymouth Congregational Church in 1980, owns and operates 13 properties, has 19 rental tenants, and provides 1000 units of housing on a Fifteen Million Dollar annual budget. The Executive Director is Paul Lambros. (www.plymouthhousing.org.)

The Plymouth model is simple: Find buildings that do not merit developers' requirements but are near public transportation and services. The group then renovates space with basic, functional units; provides on site Social Workers and Staff; and focuses on particular Homeless Groups - - the Elderly; Veterans; People with Mental Health Issues; and those living with AIDS.

I believe God would be very proud of the Blessed work of the Plymouth Congregational Church and the Plymouth

Housing Group. America needs more Churches to follow in their heavenly footsteps.

HOME OWNERSHIP:

We have too many Home Foreclosures: We must stop providing mortgages to those who cannot afford them. We must prosecute, convict, and imprison those who commit mortgage fraud. The Federal Government through FHA insurance programs must continue to support home ownership, which is the foundation of the American Way of Life.

Way too many Americans, suffering from either no or not enough income due to hard economic times, have been forced from their homes by mortgage holders. The fact that American taxpayers saved the banking and investment banking industry should encourage banks and investment banks to reduce mortgage debt to reflect actual home values in today's market. The fact that some cities are attempting to use "The Right of Imminent Domain" to take over home properties to keep people in their homes ought to be a warning that banks must do more to ameliorate the problem, or the court system may solve this nationwide human disaster. If the court system does not solve this problem, then Congress and the President must take greater action to force banks to help struggling home owners who are being thrown out of their homes on to cold, mean streets.

ILLEGAL ALIENS:

Illegal Aliens are undoubtedly among the hardest working people in this Country. Do not believe it? Try picking Grapes, Apples, Pears, Peaches or Oranges for a day, a week, a month or an entire Season. You will quickly change your mind! Try hoeing field crops: You better stock up on back pain medicine first!

*My Family worked in the grape fields of Central California during the Great Depression, when jobs were few, like now. During the 1930's my Dad took a trip to the Wenatchee Valley to pick apples when he could not get a logging job because so many men were out of work in the Country. (Sound familiar?) Dad said that picking apples was harder work for **HIM** than working as a logger, which is very hard, physical work.*

As long as the United States allows Mexico (Yes, I said allows!) to continue to be the land of the ultra rich and very poor with no Middle class, poor Mexicans will seek greater economic opportunity in the United States, even risking their lives to come here illegally. If the United States can spend trillions of dollars in Iraq and Afghanistan to Nation Build, the United States can certainly work with the Mexican Government to create a Middle Class in Mexico. Of course, it wouldn't hurt if they worked to rebuild the Middle class in the United States at the same time!

It is common sense that if the poor in Mexico had genuine opportunities for a better way of life in their home country, most would not leave their Loved Ones to risk their lives while crossing the Boarder illegally.

In the case of illegal aliens, Congress should quit playing Party Politics; Put a program in place to allow those who have come here illegally a fair and reasonable path to US Citizenship. Some Illegal Aliens, who have been here for years, have had children born in the United States, US Citizens! The Republican Party should be ashamed of itself. Abraham Lincoln must be turning over in his grave with disgust over the political turmoil in Washington D.C. Of course, I am not sure if some Republicans even know who Abraham Lincoln was, or his political philosophy. Let there be no doubt: I am a Political Independent. I just want the problems of our great Country solved with justice for all and common sense as a guide.

The Illegal Alien problem will continue to plague the United States until we definitely close the Boarder to illegal entry. Use the US Military, if necessary. Use the E – Verify employment system and penalize Companies who do not comply. Finally, treat those here now with justice and human decency, for heavens sake; let these good hard working people have a genuine opportunity to become US Citizens.

INFRASTRUCTURE:

We have Dangerous, Crumbling Infrastructure: Experts say traffic delays caused by poor roads cost The United States an estimated fifty billion dollars annually. Car crashes due to poor road maintenance cost another estimated two hundred and twenty billion dollars annually. It is claimed each time we invest one billion dollars in infrastructure almost twenty thousand construction jobs are created. The American Society of Civil Engineers estimates that disorder caused by bad infrastructure will amount to three trillion dollars lost in GDP by 2020. Let's rebuild America now!

INTERNET:

The Internet is a gift from God to mankind. It is the 21st Century Tree of Knowledge. Like the Biblical version, the Internet is filled with the fruit of good and evil.

The challenge for the world, and the United States especially, is to educate users to know the difference between the two. Free will works against the naive and the ignorant who believe that all sites and the people behind them are honest citizens who treat others fairly.

Some in the internet industry detest Government Regulation: If greed, larceny and cruelty could be eliminated from the face of the Earth, perhaps adult oversight with severe legal penalties for hurting or stealing from other people would not be necessary.

Thank God some leaders of computer and internet innovation have used their fortunes to help mankind throughout the world: Mr. and Mrs Bill and Melinda Gates; Mr. Paul Allen and Mr. Jeff and MacKenzie Bezos are just a few. How lucky the world is to be the recipient of such philanthropy.

ISRAEL:

Israel, America's Ally In The Middle East: Arabs in the Middle East (Most of whom are good peace - loving people, I suspect) must understand that the United States Government will never allow the State of Israel to be destroyed: Any serious attempt to eliminate the State of Israel will be met with a violent military reaction from the United States. I am not of the Jewish faith, but I would give my life today and always to save the Jewish State. Israel is a bulwark for peace and a very dependable American ally. The United States, however, must continue to work diligently to give the Palestinians a State of their own, as difficult as that quest may prove for Diplomats.

JAPANESE – AMERICAN CITIZENS:

American Citizens owe a big "Sorry" for what happened to Japanese – American Citizens on the West Coast during World War II: These loyal Americans were uprooted from their homes and farms in Washington, Oregon and California and shipped to "Internment Camps" in other States. (Concentration camps without the ovens; although many good people died because of the heat in the summer desert sun and the freezing winter cold.) What a travesty of justice against beautiful people whose only crime was they looked like some of the enemy. Many of these American Citizens never regained their property after the War.

The United States Government payment of reparation almost 50 years later was a small price for the taxpayer to pay for the disgusting treatment of these fine Americans. In most cases, the payment did not cover the total material loss; in any case, it did not erase heartbreaking memories.

While selling for the Procter and Gamble Distribution Company in Wyoming, monthly I would drive by and occasionally visit the remains of the Hart Mountain Relocation Camp between the cities of Cody and Powell. During a cold, Wyoming Winter that Camp must have been a very harsh environment in which to live. The United States Government treatment of these outstanding Japanese – Americans was appalling. Americans should make sure nothing like this terrible act ever happens again to another group of ethnic U.S. Citizens.

All Americans should honor the gallant courage displayed on World War II Battlefields by the All Japanese–American U.S. Army 442nd Regimental Combat Team. These men were a blessing to our Country and played a very important role in defeating the Nazis in Italy, France and Germany. Their combat exploits were remarkable. I wonder what must have been going through their minds when these brave Soldiers thought of how their Loved Ones were being treated in the "Internment Camps" back home!

The United States Army All Japanese-American 442nd Regimental Combat Team is considered to be the most heavily decorated Infantry Regiment in the History of the

U.S. Army: Eight Presidential Unit Citations; twenty one Congressional Medal Of Honor Recipients; and 9,486 Purple Hearts. The official casualty rate combining KIA (Killed In Action), MIA (Missing In Action) and WIA (Wounded and Removed from Action) was 93 percent, shockingly high. What an outstanding group of courageous and loyal American soldiers these Japanese - American Citizens were. All Americans should be very proud of their heroic bravery and sacrifice.

My family was blessed to have a wonderful Japanese-American as part of our Family: My Brother-In-Law, Captain Roy Yoshimura, was married to my Sister Roberta. Raised on the Big Island of Hawaii, Roy was a Senior Captain with Northwest Airlines who flew Boeing 747's from the West Coast of The United States to Japan, China and Singapore. Unfortunately, Roy passed away several years after reaching the mandatory Federal Aviation Retirement Age of 60; we miss him immensely.

I will always remember one Sunday afternoon at my Sister and Brother-in-Law's new home, built on a private residential Airpark, a little East of Bellevue. At the time, The Goodwill Games were being held in Seattle. To support the Goodwill Games, they had welcomed a Russian Skydiver as their house guest. The Russian Skydiver along with an American Skydiver had jumped into Husky Stadium to start the Goodwill Games. One weekend during the Goodwill Games to celebrate moving into their new home, they invited friends and relatives to a Hawaiian Luau featuring Hawaiian music, Hula Dancers and a BBQ. When the Russian Skydiver learned about the upcoming

Luau, he told them about fifty Russian men and women (husbands and wives) who traveled with a group of Russian Cosmonauts (Guests of The Boeing Company) to maintain the aircraft which brought the Russians to America from Russia. The Skydiver said these men and women were stuck at a Seattle Hotel with nothing to do and no spending money (Upon arrival each was given a ten dollar bill and told "Have fun in America!".) The Russian Skydiver asked, "Could these people attend the Luau as well?" Roy and Roberta quickly said: "Absolutely."

What a wonderful group of people these Russian Ladies and Gentlemen were! What a grand afternoon we had! Most of the Russian guests could speak English; for those who could not, an interpreter from the Department of State in Washington, D.C. was present. The day taught me that billions of dollars had been wasted by both Countries on the Cold War. Governments may distrust one another but ordinary people do not, given the opportunity to meet one another. What a great world we might have someday, if all Government Hate, Greed and Lies can be replaced with simple Human Love, Justice and Truth.

LAW ENFORCEMENT:

Americans must always respect, honor, and support Law Enforcement Personnel: These courageous citizens are on the homeland front lines of society's crimes. Without laws and the dedicated public servants who put their lives daily at risk to enforce them, life in the United States would be chaos.

It may interest you to know that our Family has roots in law enforcement: Grandpa was a part-time Town Policeman in Missouri; Uncle Earl was Sheriff of Lewis County, Washington for twelve years; and Uncle Cliff was a Security Official in Washington State.

Because of the problem of brutality on the part of some police officers, I would encourage the law enforcement community across America to follow with great interest the recent change in new recruit curriculum at the Washington State Police Academy under the direction of the Washington State Criminal Justice Training Commission. Ms. Sue Rahr, former Sheriff of King County and a 33 year veteran of Law Enforcement, is the Executive Director.

A recent example of outstanding reporting in The Seattle Times told how training at the Academy of new police recruits has shifted away from creating "Police Warriors in a Military Mold" to fashioning "Guardians of Communities." Enforcement is not the goal; it is just the tool. It is just one part of the job which includes helping people. Ms. Rahr's training model is based upon Plato's "The Republic" which maintains Guardians are gentle with Citizens but fierce with enemies. Director Rahr hopes to alter police culture statewide by teaching "Guardian Principles" to department field trainers and police leaders. "Until 'Guardian Principles' permeate the entire police family, we will not change some police behavior on the street long term." says Director Sue Rahr. The "Guardian Principle" philosophy sounds like a timely solution to police brutality wherever it exists, including on the streets of what most consider a very decent city, Seattle.

MANDATES, CHOICES, AND OPTIONS:

Americans dislike being told they "MUST" do something; we like the freedom of choice. Sometimes life with others, however, requires what is best for all, rather than just for one individual. Rules and regulations are necessary for Civil Society: Driving 50 MPH in a School Zone is foolish and unsafe – innocent children could be hurt or killed; thus, mature drivers slow down; irresponsible idiots cause accidents and get traffic tickets. Likewise, to make a medical insurance system work for all, the young and healthy must purchase health insurance though they may be just subject to accidents, relatively free from sickness. In time however, young people grow older, with a greater likelihood for illness and, of course, always facing the risk of an accident.

If the Affordable Care act has problems, Congress and the President must provide solutions! Just stop the Petty Party Politics of Obstruction. A study of American History will show that Presidents Franklin Delano Roosevelt, Harry S. Truman, and Lynden B. Johnson had the same problems of political objection and legislative turmoil in attempting to pass their Social Security and Medicare programs. Cries of "Socialism, Communism, and Redistribution of Income" rang throughout the land by Right Wing Republicans, Dixiecrats and the ultra rich in those days as well. *I say to all the paid hucksters in Washington D.C. who now are trying to take away these programs from Seniors who badly need these two programs: Forget the Veterans Bonus March on Washington, D.C. in 1932; Forget the Civil Rights March on Washington in 1963; or the Million Man March in 1995! If the Right Wing Conservatives and the ultra rich coerce others to take away or reduce Medicare and Social Security Payments, the Congress and the President could see a* **Mega – Million March of Seniors on Washington, D.C.** *Remember most Seniors are more than able to walk or roll their wheel chairs down Pennsylvania Avenue. Never forget: Not all Seniors suffer from Alzheimer's or Dementia; they have long memories; most are very honest and conscientious; and Seniors will use their* **VOTE** *to show their Displeasure as well as their Thanks in future elections!*

Under the umbrella of The Affordable Care Act, perhaps U.S. Citizens could have more health insurance options from which to choose: Medicare for the aged; Medicaid for the poor; an optional Single Payer Government run program for all ages; Private Insurance Companies for those citizens who absolutely believe private enterprise is the best bargain and **NO Insurance** for those who wish to pay hospital and medical bills **out of their own pocket**. (The Wealthy) If a patient suffering from illness or an accident enters a hospital with **NO Proof** of health insurance, or other means of payment, that individual should be refused care, unless the hospital has a Charity Program in place to serve humanity at **NO Charge**. Irresponsibility should **NO Longer** be rewarded by the American Taxpayer. Let a Church Charity Hospital provide free care to that segment of the population that refuses to act responsibly. American taxpayers have run out of patience with those who can afford to purchase Health Insurance but wish to go through life "Freeloading" off fellow Americans.

NATIONAL CONSTITUTIONAL CONVENTION:

If our Leaders remain in legislative "Gridlock", then Article Five of the United States Constitution must be used to hold a National Constitutional Convention to propose and Vote on Constitutional Amendments: If the majority thinks necessary, The United States Constitution must be amended to create, among other issues, Congressional Term Limits, As Politically Equable Congressional Districts as possible, a Balanced Budget, and a Federal Initiative Program which would allow private citizens across America to pass a badly needed law when Congress and the President will not. President Thomas Jefferson said, America should have a revolution every twenty years. A mandatory National Convention every twenty years sounds perfect to me.

NATIONAL DEBT:

The single greatest crisis facing our Country is the horrible almost 20 trillion dollar National Debt. I am certain our enemies are laughing all the way to their banks. America is being brought to its economic knees without our adversaries firing a single cannon in anger.

We must bring our Troops home from around the World and put our economic house in order. World War II has been over for almost seventy years; the Korean War over sixty. The United States must stop giving China, Japan, Korea and Germany access to our domestic markets without reciprocal trade dollar for dollar. We must stop borrowing money from China to operate our government; we must live within our economic means. Politicians must stop blaming Senior entitlements for the National Debt. I personally have never met one single Senior who did not need every penny of his or her Social Security check to live on. Remember, Seniors on Medicare do not control Hospital Prices or Health Professional fees.

Don't give me that Wyoming Cowboy Bob and North Carolina Tarheel Terry malarkey about how the fault is caused by greedy Seniors: Social Security and Medicare! Seniors haven't "stolen" money from the Social Security Trust fund—politicians have; Seniors don't set Hospital Prices, Medical Fees or Order Tests—Healthcare Professionals do. If The United States: Stops wasting money on Foreign Wars we don't HAVE to fight; stops wasting money on politically motivated Boondoggles; applies the Social Security Tax on ALL INCOME, (Municipal Bond Interest, Capital Gains as well as Earned), and substantially raises Income Taxes on the wealthy Top 20 per cent of our population, there will be plenty of Social Security money to take care of all Retirees, pay the Hospital and Medical Bills of all Senior Sick and Dying and *probably leave LEFTOVER FUNDS TO HELP PAY OFF THE NATIONAL DEBT. By the way, I wonder how much retirement income that Wyoming Cowboy Bob gets as a result of having been a US Senator—I suspect it's a lot more than most Seniors receive from Social Security. Also, I thought I heard Wyoming Cowboy Bob in Seattle bragging about how business smart and financially well off his Collegiate Honcho Buddy North Carolina Tarheel Terry is. Seems the man made $300 million dollars when he sold his Company. Strange isn't it if true, I haven't heard North Carolina Tarheel Terry, WHO IS SO CONCERNED ABOUT THE NATIONAL DEBT, say that he is giving his beloved United States $290 million dollars of his huge fortune, just to be applied to paying off the National Debt! Wealthy Prophets and Political Seers from Washington, D.C. are great for figuring out how the poor and the middle class are chiefly at fault for our National Debt. It truly seems like these over educated Carnival Barkers delight in figuring out how the poor and the middle class can and must pay the Nation's bills (or do without), while the politicians and the wealthy protect their own family financial nest. I have real questions why these professional pitchmen, who I suspect are well paid or at least financially supported by a Non-Profit Foundation which in turn is funded by a Wall Street Multi-Billionaire, travel the Country, thumping the drum of national bankruptcy. These two men of economic calamity sing the tune of national woe as written by funded scholars of the Multi-Billionaire. The problem is their so called facts are based upon erroneous data which was developed by Harvard*

University Economists. Other academics after analyzing the data, found serious errors in the work: Coding errors, selective exclusion of available data, and unconventional weighing of summary statistics which led to serious errors that represent the relationship between public debt and GDP growth among 20 advanced economies in the Post – War period. So much for what these two Shills have to say. It's just another nasty attack by the top 20 Percent of the wealth in this Country on the bottom 80 Per Cent of Americans. The Geezer Billionaire should just take his Multi – Billion Dollar fortune, give it to the US Government with the proviso that it can only be applied to the National debt, then retire to a Nursing Home somewhere. PLEASE, JUST STOP PICKING ON SENIORS!

Oh and one other brilliant thought, Wyoming Cowboy Bob should have a heart to heart talk with his Wyoming Buddy, the Former Vice President Dick Chaney, now that Mr. Chaney has a new heart. Wyoming Cowboy Bob should persuade Mr. Chaney that it would be great if Mr. Chaney would pay the US Treasury a hundred million dollars or so of the grand sum he made off his Stocks while certain companies were taking the American Taxpayer for every dollar it could through contracts in Iraq during the Iraq War. Yes I know: Mr. Chaney and his Stocks were in Trust. But, rest assured, the Former Vice President went to bed each night during the Iraq War with a big smile on his face, especially knowing his two daughters were not in harm's way in a combat zone. As I have said before, the rich and the political elite have no objections to sending the *children of other parents to die in a Combat Zone for a war the United States did not have to fight - - just not **their** Children!*

The United States must stop thinking that we have to be the World's policeman. **The United States is Broke; we do not have funds for such luxury.** We should totally stay out of the Civil Wars of other Countries. I do not remember reading about other Countries who fought for the North or the South during our horrible, but necessary, Civil War (or War Between The States, if you are so inclined).

Our President and Congress must attack the National Debt of the United States like we fought World War II: Total Annihilation ! Our future totally depends upon the economic well being of The United States. We must substantially tax the top 20 percent of our population who own 80 percent of all private wealth. During World War II (1944 and 1945) the top marginal tax rate was 94%; from 1940 to 1963 the top marginal tax rate was above 80 %. From the Reagan years of the 80's to today, the top marginal tax rates match the years of the 1920's, just prior to the Great Depression.

It never hurts to repeat that we must stop wasting tax dollars by trying to "Buy Friends" through Foreign Aid; we must also try to eliminate as much waste as possible in Government Departments and Programs. All Americans must be involved to solve our National Debt Crisis: The ultra wealthy (3 %) , Wealthy (17%), Middle class and the poor (80 %). (Unfortunately, it has reached a point in America that it is almost impossible to separate the Middle Class from the Poor!) Obviously, those who possess the greatest ability to pay the most, **must!** Time to solve our National Debt Crisis is running out: The Golden Goose of the wealthy twenty percent of Americans will soon lay a rock brick, if the bottom 80% are not allowed a fair opportunity to make a decent living to start paying their FAIR share of income taxes.

NATIONAL SECURITY;

National Security of the United States should be one of the most important agendas for all Americans. After my Military Service, I have always said that sometimes the only people in the World who do not know what the United States Government is doing around the World are the United States Citizens themselves. Certainly the people who bear the brunt of some of our Government's activities know what is being done to them: Some activities are absolutely necessary and heroic, while some are not; and some have been cruel to others and foolish and costly to the wholesome reputation of the United States in the eyes of our fellow world citizens.

To function in the 8th Data Processing Unit during my tour of Duty in the US Army, I was required to have a "Top Secret" US Army Military Clearance. In my case, the clearance was unnecessary for me to do my job of very little importance; I did, however, witness US Army Personnel working in an environment where a Top Security Clearance was vital to the computer work of my fellow Soldiers.

A funny thing happened to my Mother as a result of an 8th DPU Company request for a US Army Top Secret Clearance for me. A Federal Bureau of Investigation Agent arrived in my home town to ask questions of key people in the Community about my background, integrity and loyalty to the United States Constitution. After knocking on my Parents door in error, the FBI Agent asked my Mother if she knew a US Army Private by the name of James A. Nelson? My Mother replied, "I should. He is my son. I gave birth to him." The FBI Interview ended abruptly!

I believe that a more thorough background check of both Private Bradley Manning and Mr. Edward Snowden should have been accomplished, prior to giving each a Top Security Clearance. Perhaps a more complete screening process would have shown both men unqualified to work with United States Top Secret Information, preventing their ultimate disloyalty to our Country.

The United States Army should be ashamed of the Bradley Manning affair. There is no doubt Private Manning broke his oath to the United States Government and the United States Army. He deserved to be punished; however, his Military Superiors should have handled this problem prior to his disloyalty. After reading about his Military career, any U.S. Army Veteran would know Private Manning was not proper U.S. Army material. He should **Never** have been given a National Security Clarence to work with Government Secret Documents. For me, there is ample evidence that Private Manning should have been medically discharged as unfit for duty, prior to his releasing secret information. I suspect our US Army manpower shortage is what kept Private Manning in his job in Iraq.

Mr. Edward Snowden is another matter. Obviously a very bright man, I am still amazed how he could have gained access to so much secret United States Government Information so quickly and easily. The ultimate harm remains to be seen. Perhaps the lessons to be learned from this affair are: Be careful who you hire; be careful what private emails of a friendly government you secretly read or telephone calls you intercept (Think Brazil, Germany or Mexico); and be honest, careful and wise in one's work in behalf of fellow American Citizens, for poor performance may embarrass you and your Country.

While it is too early to tell what the ultimate result of Private Manning and Mr. Snowden's crimes will be to the National Security of The United States, I must remind fellow Citizens that when the Pentagon Papers were released during the Viet Nam War by a United States Citizen, Government Officials were upset, too. The release of The Pentagon Papers led to much doubt by U.S. Citizens about why the United States ever got involved, or continued to fight, in Viet Nam. History shows that when our Government hides the truth of its activities from the People of the United States, the whole Country loses**. To Para- phrase President Ronald W. Reagan, "We must trust our Government, but verify its truthfulness at the same time."**

NEWSPAPERS;

Newspapers are the lifeblood of information for United States Citizens. The keys to Freedom, Justice and the Continuation of our Republic Of The People, By The People and For The People is a free press, unencumbered by Government interference. In recent years, the Newspaper Industry has been decimated by Broadcast and Cable Television competition in the fight for advertising revenue. Today, Internet advertising has also begun to greatly impact on Newspaper revenue.

Newspaper investigative reporting shall always be the ultimate tool for United States Citizens to learn the truth about U.S. Government activity: Federal, State, County, City, and Township. A Free Press in our Republic is a Constitutional Right; It is also a common sense necessity.

We should create a special "Information" Tax on Broadcast and Cable Television advertising as well as Internet Advertising to support Newspapers nationwide. Newspapers, in turn, can reduce their subscription prices to allow more citizens access to their valuable information. They can also afford to hire more professional reporters to research and write important articles of investigation.

United States Citizens profit greatly from both the National Public Radio and The Public Broadcasting Television Networks, supported by Taxpayers, Non-Profit Groups, listeners and viewers. Citizens gain valuable information and knowledge about their Government, Country and the World from these Institutions; their contributions to our freedom are incalculable.

Instead of creating a Public National Newspaper, our Government should support Investigative Reporting by our existing private Newspapers through funds generated by taxing Internet, Radio and Television Advertising. A financially successful private newspaper system is imperative to our freedom; the First Amendment to the Constitution of The United States has played a vital role throughout our History.

The recent acquisition of The Washington Post by Mr. Jeff Bezos, owner of the internet giant Amazon.com., is a genuine contribution to his fellow Americans. Other multi-billionaires should follow in Mr. Bezos's investment footsteps, to save our independent source of U.S. and Worldwide news and information.

NON – PROFIT GROUPS:

Too many Non-Profit Groups function in a "Black Hole" environment. I suspect some Non – Profit Groups chiefly exist to provide a legal way to deny the Federal Government a larger amount of income tax revenue: Helping others is only a side benefit. Also, some Non-Profit Groups exist chiefly to provide employment for family members, I suspect.

Yearly, Non-Profit Groups of a certain dollar value should be required to annually publish in America's newspapers a report recapping the activities of the Non-Profit Group: Financial condition, funds spent, executive salaries and future plans to help others, especially fellow Americans. Some

Non-Profit executives believe the less citizens know about a non – profit's activity the better, I suspect.

Today, I do not wish to learn just what a Non-Profit Group is doing in the rest of the World. What I would like to know is what they are doing to help fellow Americans. It is time to focus on America's problems of hunger, poverty, healthcare, unemployment and our inadequate pre-school, elementary, middle and high school education system.

We all hear and read what an outstanding Non-Profit Group the Gates Foundation is. We just might think even more highly of The Gates Foundation if we were told on an annual basis in the Daily Newspapers of the United States how these good people are helping their Fellow Americans, as well as people in other Countries! For sure, God has blessed the State of Washington, The United States Of America and The World with Mr. and Mrs. Bill and Melinda Gates and their Good and Magnanimous Friend, Mr. Warren Buffett: Their generosity to share their huge fortunes in behalf of others through humanitarian projects and medical research worldwide is a wondrous blessing for all mankind.

Finally, perhaps one of the most important contributions a few Non-Profit Groups in America can make short term is to contribute five per cent yearly of their gross dollar value to help reduce the terrible National Debt of the United States. Since in many cases, the money to create Non-Profit Foundations in the United States originated from financial activity in the United States, perhaps such a program is appropriate now because of our potential economic catastrophe due to our National Debt.

ORGANIZED LABOR:

Destruction of Organized Labor: In my lifetime the destruction of Organized Labor is disgraceful and unfortunate for America's middle class. If owners and management treated their employees with dignity and living income wages, Unions would not be necessary. The export of American middle-class jobs must be stopped. We must rebuild the economic position of middle-class families here in The United States. Organized Labor is always the answer when Wall Street and Management greed overwhelms common sense and financial decency.

In my mind today, the most powerful Unions in our Country are those involved in Transportation: Trucking, Airlines and Railroads. These Union men and women have the power to totally shut down the United States Economy, which is the only power that some management and company owners will heed, unfortunately.

The destruction of Unions in the United States started under the reign of President Ronald W. Reagan with his dispute with the Air Traffic Controllers Union (PATCO) in 1981. What a travesty of justice against the working men and women that episode was. The disagreement certainly could have been handled with greater fairness to those valuable Professional Men and Women who possessed priceless years of on the job experience. The Air Traffic Controllers did have legitimate complaints about working hours and conditions, with the safety of the flying public definitely at stake.

To assist the PATCO Strikers, the Airline Union Pilots could have refused to fly, but few chose to support the strikers. Later, Union Airline Pilots suffered losses in income and membership numbers due to Airline Company mergers: PATCO members had they not lost their jobs could have supported Pilots. I have always believed that if PATCO had chosen to strike during the Winter when Airline traffic must fly IFR (Instrument Flight Rules), which requires a large number of the 11,000 Air Traffic Controllers to be on duty at all times for safety reasons, the outcome of the strike would have been much different. However, with the PATCO Strike occurring in the summer weather of August, many of the Aircraft were able to fly VFR (Visual Flight Rules – physically looking out the window) with far fewer ATC employees needed on duty throughout the day and night.

President Ronald W. Reagan and his Gang Of Union Busters did not waste any time following an ultimatum to PATCO to end the strike: Striking PATCO members were fired! To work in Airport Control Towers to manage landings and takeoffs, the Government immediately hired back 2,000 PATCO Members who chose not to support their Union; ordered 900 United States Military Controllers to temporary duty with the Air Traffic Control System and, finally, used 3000 Federal Aviation Administration Management Personnel to keep the Air Traffic Control System running. How safe flying was for the general public was another question! Thank God, we had highly skilled Airline Pilots with great eyesight and a whole lot of good luck during that horrible Reagan Administration Union Busting ordeal!

The Nation's Airline Companies and The Air Traffic Control System continued to function. The strike was broken; PATCO destroyed. Reagan's Gang of Union Busters won; the working man and woman Lost! The ability of PATCO to force a strike settlement on Union Terms was impossible without the support of **All of America's Union Members**. Frankly, the Nation's Middle Class lost immensely with the Reagan Administration's dismantling of the PATCO Union.

For sure, the once President of The Screen Actors Guild, President Ronald W. Reagan, did not contribute to the welfare of the Union Man in America. Once President Reagan formed his California Kitchen Cabinet of multi-millionaires, he forgot his Union Roots, unfortunately. The Reagan Administration's attack on the PATCO Strike was the beginning of a 30 year attack on Unionism in America, tragically. Perhaps the Transportation Unions can play a lead role in Re-Establishing living income jobs with benefits for more of America's Middle Class: **The sooner, the better.**

"ORVILLE NUTQUEST":

TO ATTACK OUR NATIONAL DEBT, any Member of The House or Senate who lets one individual (One Citizen! One Voter!) stop the Member from increasing necessary taxes on the twenty percent of wealthy Americans who own eighty- nine percent of the Nation's private wealth should be voted from office at the first opportunity! An elected Member allegedly representing **ALL** of his constituents should not allow himself to be politically coerced by **ONE INDIVIDUAL OR ONE LOBBY GROUP** to sign a statement categorically refusing to raise taxes (The Member should refute his signature immediately, if the Member has already signed.). We cannot solve our almost twenty trillion dollar National Debt by just reducing expenditures; taxes must be substantially raised on all Citizens who can afford to pay more, especially on the wealthy top twenty percent who own 89 per cent of this Nation's private wealth.

The United States Of America is a Constitutional Republic, not an Oligarchy! It is obvious to the other eighty percent of the United States taxpayers that many of our Elected Leaders have forgotten this fact!

Soon we all must will learn this lesson, or the United States Of America as we have know it for over 200 years will disappear, I fear! Because of our horrible National Debt, time is not on our side; fortunately God is.

PROFESSIONAL , COLLEGIATE AND HIGH SCHOOL ATHLETICS:

Financial assistance from professional sports would be greatly appreciated by our schools. Team Owners and Professional Athletes would be **National Heroes,** if a small percentage of the hundreds of millions of dollars of

Professional Sport ticket and television advertising revenue was used to support America's High School competitive sports and physical education programs at all levels of High, Middle and Elementary School. All are struggling financially nationwide. Financial assistance from professional sports would be greatly appreciated by our schools. I believe financial assistance money from professional sports to High Schools would fertilize the Glorious Garden where future professional sports stars are planted and nurtured.

Collegiate Athletic Television revenue is now used to pay coaches Exorbitant Salaries and Perks and build luxurious stadiums and gymnasiums. It is way past time to use some of these funds to provide student athletes a monthly stipend to financially assist them while in school. It is not enough for College Administrators to maintain "We give them a free education." There is nothing "Free" in life. The truth is: A student athlete must study to maintain a required GPA, pass tests and courses, and persevere to graduate, all the while playing a very competitive sport throughout the year. Student athletes create and **EARN** every penny they could possibly be "granted"; they also EARN millions of dollars for Colleges and Universities through their athletic prowess. College and University Football and Basketball programs are the "Minor Leagues" for the NFL and the NBA; at the same time, Collegiate sports help build positive relationships between Colleges and Universities and the Taxpayers who, ultimately, underwrite most of the cost of our Collegiate Education System.

Additionally, it is time for College Presidents and Athletic Directors to take back control of collegiate athletics from TV Companies. Taxpayers provide the majority of the funds to operate Colleges and Universities, not the Television Industry. It is an abomination to have our outstanding College and University Presidents and other Administrators relinquish control of broadcasting rights and rules so readily: Collegiate Sports Money is certainly the Root of some abdication of responsibility on the part of those who are paid by Taxpayers to be in control.

Anyone who truly knows me should be well aware of the value I place on competitive sports at all levels of Education. Student mind and body development, Taxpayer Entertainment, and the enrichment of National Morale and Character are all worthy values created by organized sports at all levels of competition.

Colleges and Universities simply must start paying student athletes a monthly stipend and this Nation must continue to support competitive sport and physical education programs at Elementary, Middle and High Schools. A minuscule portion of professional and collegiate sports ticket and television revenue would be a terrific and reasonable resource to use for additional support. **Remember what Five Star General Of The US Army Douglas MacArthur stated: "On the fields of friendly strife are sown the seeds that on other days and other fields will bear the fruits of Victory."**

As long as I'm on the subject of the NFL, Congress and the President should demand full disclosure about the risk of brain damage by playing football. The recent program established by the NFL in conjunction with Boston University is certainly an admirable first step. I loved playing football in High School and College and found the competition very challenging. American Football is God's gift to our Country and the World: A very competitive sport which teaches courage, discipline, pride, teamwork and the will to win.

Parents, Wives, and Players need to know the true risk of brain damage involved in playing the game at all levels of competition. *Though my Wife suggests that I've suffered from brain damage for all of our 45 years of marriage, I've always believed that because I was never allowed to play tackle football until I was a Freshman in High School, I was wisely protected by my Parents and School Administrators from possible early brain injury.*

RACIAL MINORITIES:
We must never forget the terrible fight for Constitutional Freedoms and Economic Opportunities that Racial Minorities have been forced to wage throughout American History. Thank God life in the last fifty years in the United States for Racial Minorities has improved. We still have much work yet to do to see that all have equal opportunities; but we are making progress.

Throughout much of American History, Black Citizens, above all others, have been denied Freedom and Opportunity as guaranteed by the US Constitution and The Bill Of Rights.

America's History of Black Americans held in slavery is abominable. We as a Country must continue to improve life in America for our Black citizens. Love should replace hate. Creativity, Intelligence and Courage are not determined by the color of one's skin. *I learned that fact very quickly during my service with the Unites States Army. I pray that Common Sense and Faith will change some Minds and Hearts for the better.*

We must never forget that Non – Whites have contributed immensely to the development of our great Country. Since the Revolutionary War, many have given their lives in America's Wars to keep our Country free. *Years ago, I served with many brave, honorable and very patriotic Non -White Military Men and Women. It would be an Honor to serve with them again. When I served in the US Army, Black men and women and other minorities played a very important role in my life; I can never thank them enough for their Leadership, Respect and Friendship. My memories of them will last a lifetime and are invaluable.*

RELIGION:

Some Religions have Serious Problems: It is not my place to criticize the religious institutions of other Americans, except when American laws are broken by their members. Religious Leaders should be ashamed of some Clergy activity. The failure to correct problems of immorality is unconscionable as well as illegal in most instances. Religious Leaders should always set a high standard by living in accordance with God's word, The

Bible. Those who wish to replace our civil and criminal laws with anything that is not based on the Constitution and Bill of Rights of the United States of America should be immediately stopped. Sharia law may be appropriate for other countries, but not for the United States of America.

RESEARCH AND DEVELOPMENT:

We must increase Research and Development Investment: Our creativity and ingenuity has enabled the United States to lead the world in innovation. Our expenditures have fallen to a point where we now rank ninth in the world. We must not financially starve the originality that will improve the lives of all.

REVERSE MORTGAGE:

To Many Seniors this program is a true blessing. Today, I have a part-time job I consider a noble calling: Helping my fellow seniors ease their financial burden during the last years of life through the acquisition of a HUD / FHA / HECM (Home Equity Conversion Mortgage, otherwise known as a Reverse Mortgage). This outstanding financial tool allows Seniors to use some of their home equity to either stop a conventional mortgage payment or create funds for emergencies through a line of credit without a monthly payment. The Reverse Mortgage permits Seniors to remain in their own homes, which is where most of us prefer to live out our lives.

The President, Congress, and HUD / FHA must be praised for their support of the Reverse Mortgage Program. It must be expanded, however, by lowering the age of qualification to help more Seniors use this retirement tool. To prevent a younger partner from being forced from the home when the older partner dies, Life Insurance should be purchased when a younger partner removes his / her name from the home title to make the FHA /HECM formula work. Proceeds from the policy can then be used to buy down the mortgage debt to allow the younger partner to qualify for a Reverse Mortgage Loan, when the older partner passes.

Because of the age difference between my wife and me, I was required to remove her name from our home title to make the FHA/ HECM formula work (age of the youngest partner, amount of the existing conventional mortgage if any, and FHA Appraised Home Value). I told my Wife that when I die, she could use my Life Insurance proceeds to reduce the amount of the existing FHA/HECM loan to qualify for her own Reverse Mortgage. Of course, my gorgeous, humorous wife said, **"Maybe, maybe not. I might keep the life insurance money, sell the house for whatever I can get out of it, and then after paying off your debt, go find a younger man with more money than I have!" I told her, "More power to you. Either I will be flying my airplane "Call Me Lucky" with Yokie as my CoPilot up to an Airport in Heaven OR I will be shoveling coal down below with some of the most sexy,**

voluptuous ladies a man can imagine, and, frankly, I won't give a damn, to paraphrase Rhett Butler, a handsome Southern Gentleman from a Famous Book of Unforgettable Southern Fiction: 'Gone With The Wind' *." A favorite Book of my fifth grade teacher Miss Charlotte Heart, my Mother and my self — after I grew up and was allowed to read such a fabulous love story! Mom said one time when we were discussing this beautiful Literary Work Of Authentic American History: "Jim, that Book was written by a Woman, Ms. Margaret Mitchell—it had to be. You must understand there is a lot of both Scarlett O'Hara and Melanie Hamilton in every Woman. The problem is too many men don't want a strong Woman who can stand on her own two feet with her head held high, while fighting life's battles. All too many men want a Woman who will just take orders, bow and stoop to every foolish command a man gives, say please and thank you for every little morsel of food and sex a man provides, and keep her mouth shut while remaining in the background. You're going to learn in time that Women have minds, too—many brilliant; that most Women are far more loving and forgiving than men; and also, Women will persevere until the end, as well as, if not better than men . Women proved their Metal during World War II, both overseas and here at home. For sure one of these days, Women will play a greater role in running our Government at all levels of Office. In time, we will even have a Woman President. I may not live to see it, but that's one event that will come to pass perhaps in your lifetime,* *believe me. One of these days though, being a typical Male who thinks he's God's Gift to Women, your comeuppance is coming, I fear! Knowing how important it is to have a mate you can love, respect and support, I do pray that you will find your self a strong Woman who can act for the both of you in your absence. A Woman who also has the intelligence and kindness to overlook your inherited Male Vanity when it shows its face." Guess what? I finally found such a Woman and Mom was right about my Vanity as well: My tenacious and loving Wife, Marylil, says "it has shown its face many times."*

The American taxpayer will save millions of dollars, if not billions, by allowing Seniors to pay for their lodging by remaining in their own homes. In the past, many Seniors have been moved to nursing homes with the enormous cost paid by the American Taxpayer through Medicaid: four thousand to eight thousand dollars a month! Some additional thought must be given to help those Seniors with Reverse Mortgages who require financial assistance to pay for homeowners insurance, real estate taxes and routine maintenance. Whatever the cost, it will be less expensive than paying for nursing home care through Medicaid, if an available bed can even be found! To assist those Seniors without immediate Family who choose to remain in their own homes, Medicare Homecare Services must be expanded to help those whose health has severely deteriorated prior to death.

Additionally, if the younger partner does not qualify for private company life insurance due to health issues at his / hers age, the Federal Government should offer "A Special Life

Insurance Policy for the FHA/HECM Program", just as the Federal Government does through FEMA for homeowners living on a flood plain. The Insurance Industry may sell a policy to make a commission from Flood Insurance, but private Insurance Companies do not subject themselves to the risk of loss from floods. The Federal Government alone offers Flood Insurance which Private Industry will not offer due to loss History. Remember: The HECM Program allows a Senior to provide his own shelter at his / her expense; that is a much cheaper deal for the taxpayer than Nursing Home Care paid by Medicaid! (i.e., The Taxpayer!)

One aspect of the Reverse Mortgage Industry that I absolutely despise is the atrocious Telephone Call Centers that badger Seniors at all hours of the day and night. The practice of selling a Reverse Mortgage to a Senior strictly over the telephone should be banned immediately. (However, setting an In Home Appointment by telephone for a Loan Officer to visit and explain the Program to the Senior is perfectly legitimate.) If a Mortgage Company does not have enough respect for a Senior to send a Loan Originator to a Seniors' home to explain the advantages of a FHA /HECM in person across the Kitchen / Dining Room Table, or in a Seniors Living Room, that Mortgage Company should be banned forever from doing business in the HUD / FHA HECM field. Seniors well deserve all the respect they have earned through a lifetime of service to their Country. To be insulted by Unscrupulous, Drummer, Corporate employees is just ridiculous. If HUD does not put a stop to this grievous practice of totally selling an FHA/

HECM Reverse Mortgage over the telephone without a Loan Originator from the mortgage company going to the Senior's home, Congress and the President should!

SOCIAL SECURITY; MEDICARE:

We have yet to act upon Social Security and Medicare Reform: We must eliminate Social Security eligibility for well - off Senior recipients who have no financial need for Social Security; if necessary to guarantee solvency, raise the earnings amount to which Social Security taxes apply to include **ALL** income, Municipal Bond Interest, Capitol Gains as well as earned, and return funds stolen from the so - called Invisible "Lock Box" to which too many politicians have had a key. For economic fairness to Seniors, Social Security annual cost of living adjustments should be based upon the new US Bureau of Labor Statistics — "consumer price index for the elderly" — rather than the "chained consumer price index." The first reflects *Actual* spending changes as citizens grow older (increases in health care and housing costs). The second encompasses the *total* United States population where spending decisions are largely based on cost savings.

We must stop blaming Seniors for the high cost of Medicare. Change pricing mechanisms by hospitals and professionals, and negotiate drug prices with the pharmaceutical industry. A sad commentary on the health system of The United States is that according to the World Health Organization we rank

37th of 191 Countries in the World. (Yes I know, rankings are disputed by Health Professionals and others. One fact I do know is that our Health Care System can be improved for the good of all Citizens.) We currently spend about eight thousand dollars annually per person on Health Care compared to a little over four thousand dollars annually by our neighbor, Canada. A further horrible indictment of our existing medical system is that it is estimated that over one hundred thousand patients die each year due to medical errors. Some experts claim the high cost of Medicare could be reduced by almost thirty percent – perhaps as much as seven hundred billion dollars — if unnecessary services, inflated administrative costs and fraud could be eliminated, or at least substantially reduced.

Recently, a major drug company announced a new drug to combat Rheumatoid Arthritis: The cost for a Medicare **SINGLE** *patient is $2,055 per month or $24,666 per year. Four years ago my Wife was diagnosed with a serious case of Rheumatoid Arthritis. Some said she would soon be ready for a wheelchair. I read a newspaper column in the Seattle Times called: "The People's Pharmacy." I also purchased a book by the same authors in which we found two recipes that have worked a miracle for her. The* **First**: *One package of Certo (liquid fruit pectin) mixed in a 64 ounce bottle of grape juice. Drink 6 ounces every day.* **The Second**: *One - 10 ounce package of raisins, marinated overnight in Gin. Take two teaspoons every day. The cost for these two recipes is less than thirty dollars per month! Since these recipes are food,* *for most patients there are no side effects, which may not be the case with prescription drugs.*

Today, my Wife is pain free with few symptoms of Rheumatoid Arthritis. The severe pain in her feet, hands, and joints is gone. She continues to enjoy a totally pain-free life, thanks entirely to these two remarkable recipes found in The People's Pharmacy. She says she will never stop taking these items! Every Senior should read The People's Pharmacy weekly column in their local newspaper or purchase the book "The People's Pharmacy" by: Joe and Terry Graedon, available online at www.thepeoplespharmacy.com. This marvelous book has valuable information about folk medicine regimens for many diseases and ailments. Statements in this book are from people who actually use these remedies to combat their diseases. Will the remedies work for all patients? Probably not. But again, it is worth a try. At a cost of less than thirty dollars monthly compared to $2,055 monthly for a prescription drug, why would one hesitate to try this inexpensive regimen?

It is high time Seniors be allowed to use simple folk medicine healing agents paid for by Medicare, especially if the products are cheaper and may heal without side effects. Sounds like a winner for all involved, except the drug industry, of course. At a monthly cost of $2,055, I do not believe the drug industry is spending too much time worrying about saving the American taxpayer money. Why should the American taxpayer lose any sleep over the objections of the prescription drug lobby?

One more thought, if the Private Drug Industry is no longer going to research to develop new antibiotic drugs to *combat current drug resistant bugs, the National Institute of Health must take action immediately: **Funded by a special tax on Drug Industry Gross Sales Dollars.***

By the way, if you think I am anti - pharmaceutical industry, please think again. The United States Pharmaceutical Industry is one of the world's greatest centers of innovation to combat human disease and illness. Without their products, our health-care costs would sky-rocket and patients would either suffer needlessly or die prematurely. In the early 1970's, I published a unique health-care journal in the United States: "The Health Team Approach," for all members of the Health-Care Team. Once, my Wife and I had as a house guest the President of the Advertising Agency Williams Douglas Mc Adams —then one of the largest agencies in the Pharmaceutical Advertising Business. Their primary client was Hoffmann - La Roche, makers of Valium and Librium, which at the time were two of the best - selling prescription drugs. I will never forget what the Gentleman told me: "If the pharmaceutical industry gave away all of its products, Nelson, it would reduce the total American health-care bill by only ten percent." The same is essentially true today as well, I suspect.

Thus, if the Country wishes to find substantial savings in our health-care system, it must look elsewhere in medical care and hospital costs, not the Pharmaceutical Industry. I simply state that to save American taxpayers money, we should first try the least expensive treatment available which may provide a patient relief, even if it is just a much cheaper food product or simply a better diet.

SPACE PROGRAM;

We must continue to invest funds in the Space Program:

While selling toothpaste for the Proctor and Gamble Distribution Company in South Dakota, Nebraska and Wyoming, I had a weekly radio interview program called "Black Hills Today" on a station in Rapid City, South Dakota. One of my guests was USAF Colonel Frank Borman, one of the original NASA Astronauts. I asked him, "Why, after landing a man on the moon, should America continue to invest tax dollars in the United States Space Program?" He answered, "Because the United States Space Program is the greatest source of innovation in the world, short of war." His answer has always made great common sense to me; what an intelligent, articulate, courageous American Hero is United States Air Force Colonel Frank Borman!

Some of my other memorable Guests on "Black Hills Today" were Country Music Stars: Roy Acuff and Loretta Lynn; Mr. Joe Kirkwood of Hollywood Movie Star Joe Palooka Fame; United States Senator Karl Mundt; National Political Columnist Drew Pearson; Hollywood Music Legend Lawrence Welk; and the Famous Western Singing Group The Sons Of The Pioneers.

"Black Hills Today" was simply an example of my Self Education. I certainly admit though that my "On The Job Training" was a far cry from a Four Year Field of Study at Harvard University, The University Of Washington or even Valley City State Teachers College in North Dakota.

I was pleased to find that my Guests were generous with their time, kindness and courtesy. By asking somewhat intelligent questions and actually listening to the answers of my Guests, the Listeners and I learned a great deal about their lives. What a thrill and an education it was for me to meet these Famous, G ood and Talented People.

WALL STREET:

We have too much Wall Street Bank Mischief: Investigate, arrest, prosecute, and imprison those convicted of fraud, theft, or any other investment banking dishonesty. Non – probationary sentences of a minimum of five years is absolutely necessary. Prosecutors in some States have put the poor in jail for stealing $20.00. Admittedly in part because a weapon was used in the crime, I suspect. However, thieves on Wall Street using a "computer cannon" have stolen millions of dollars and few have served one day behind bars! Stockholders and other investors must be protected against those on Wall Street who will steal precious retirement dollars from others.

During the 1980's and 1990's, deregulation allowed Saving and Loan Institutions to act like banks. Without government oversight, depositors were left unprotected and excessive risk ran rampant. By the mid 1990's one third of the Savings and Loans had failed. Ultimately, the cost to the taxpayers was one hundred and twenty four billion dollars. However, the Justice Department did its job, taking the unscrupulous thieves to court: Convictions sent over one thousand people to jail.

To date, the same claim cannot be said for the Justice Department's handling of the deregulation allowed sub-prime mortgage debacle. With almost five hundred banks closed, and some say an estimated cost to the taxpayers of almost thirteen trillion dollars, and a slow return to economic stability with full employment, taxpayers are still waiting for the Justice Department to take ALL of the Wall Street Bandits to Federal Court. The Attorney General and his Crew Of Legal Bull Dogs must prosecute and, hopefully, convict these thieves; Judges must lock them up and throw away the key for a non – probationary period for at least five years. Plus, the Justice Department must "Clawback" huge undeserved executive salaries by seeking large fines, in some cases amounting to hundreds of millions of dollars.

Statue of limitation laws should be voided for these Wall Street economic crimes against the American People. Wealthy criminals should not be allowed to escape investigation, prosecution, conviction and, ultimately, penalty. To protect against future Wall Street financial chicanery, Congress and the President must immediately re-instate an updated version of the Glass – Segal Law of the 1930's.

We must tax capital gains at the same rate as ordinary income. We must also tax Municipal Bonds Interest like ordinary income. Income, regardless of it's source, is income. pure and simple. When investment income is not taxed like ordinary income, the United States lays the ground work for why twenty percent of the population ends up owning eighty nine percent of the private wealth in the United States.

I repeat — The United States is a Republic, not an Oligarchy.

Recently in the Seattle Times, a full page ad ran, touting the value of investing in Municipal Bonds. The ad stated in Huge, Bold Print three reasons for investing in Municipal Bonds. (**ONE**) potential (**?**) Safety of Principal. (**TWO**) potential (?) Regular Predictable Income. and (**THREE**) potential (?) **TRIPLE Tax – Free Income.** (The question marks are **mine**!).

Though the Wall Street Wizards will state otherwise, I doubt if a small tax on Municipal Bond Interest would reduce purchases by the rich. If so, too bad! The rich are too rich now!

Few Americans are financially able to invest in Municipal Bonds. Rich Investors can afford to pay taxes on Municipal Bond Income to the United States Treasury, reducing our National Debt while making our country a more equal Nation. *Never forget what the Author Mr. George Orwell said in his book "Animal Farm": "All pigs are equal, but some pigs are more equal than others." Today, the United States has reached a very "PIGGISH point in our economic history. My Father enjoyed reading "Animal Farm", when I brought the book home from College. Dad said, "Never forget, Jim, greed destroys men and Countries!" My Dad was a very smart man with great common sense! He was very serious when he made that statement.* I truly believe the rich top 20 per cent of our population think the rest of us United States Citizens are pure stupid. And perhaps we are….or have been. With the power of Elections and the Vote, the rich top 20 per cent have to be taken to President Ronald Reagan's "Famous Woodshed"! The "Trickle Down Theory" for the poor and the middle class has proven to be nothing more than a "Gusher-Up" reality for the rich top 20 per cent of Americans! Thirty years later, "Reaganomics" have become "Trickanomics" for 80 per cent of US Citizens.

I pray that most of those working on Wall Street are honest men and women. Someone once said, "The Root of all Evil is Money." I have always thought, "NO, the Root of SOME EVIL is Money." Money to operate society is vitally necessary; it is how one earns money that determines whether people are honest or not; it is how people use money that determines whether all Citizens are helped or not.

WAR:

History shows there is no such thing as a "Little", "Quick" or "Easy" War. The United States should fight wars of total annihilation only when our National Security is truly threatened by other Countries or Terrorists, internally or externally. This is still the greatest, most powerful, most benevolent Country in the World. If we mind our business and let others mind their own affairs, regardless of how awful another Government may be, our Country will be much better off. Whether The United States likes it or not, as bad as it may be, there are Countries where only a benevolent dictator can keep different religious or ethnic groups from killing one another continuously. World History shows there is no such thing as a "Little", "Quick" or "Easy" War. **The only people who believe that nonsense are those who want someone else to do the fighting. (And, certainly not with THEIR Children!)**

WOMAN'S CHOICE:

A Woman's choice is the Law of the Land: If organized religion wishes to outlaw all abortions, then require organized religion to pay the one hundred and fifty thousand dollars or more it costs to raise an unwanted child to adulthood. Do not expect taxpayers to continue to pay the bill. Let there be no doubt: I do not believe in late term abortions. Contraceptive programs, however, should be readily available at little or no cost to those who cannot afford them. A birth control pill is less emotionally traumatizing than an unwanted baby: Cheaper for The Taxpayer, too! Mandatory sex education classes should be available for all students in Junior High and High School. **Abstinence until marriage is still a very wise decision; it is just not a very realistic policy for ALL young people in this day and age of explicit sex on the Internet, Television and in the Movies.**

Frankly, I truly have never understood why some men object to a vasectomy rather than have children they cannot properly care for financially, or socially. *Truly, I understand why men want and like sex. Once I learned in my 20's how much fun it was, I developed a love for sex with women, as well. Fortunately, I married a "Marilyn Monroe – Look–A–Like" who thinks it is pretty good, too. But after four children, I had a vasectomy because I knew we could not afford any more children.* Of course, I could say something similar to women: After you have had whatever number of children you and your husband can afford to take care of, get your tubes tied. Sex without having to worry about getting pregnant might be fun for you as well! Your religion objects to such a procedure? Then, let your Church Treasury pay to raise your children, if you cannot, or you and your husband will not. Just do not ask the American Taxpayer to continue to pay for your immature, careless and costly sexual habits.

Our Government has no actual shortage of income. Our problems I suspect are those of Greed, Waste and Foolish Allocation of Funds. While we are reducing our National Debt, our Government must do more with less and the private sector must create jobs where those with less can **earn** more.

One of the richest men in America, Mr. Warren Buffett, has indicated America's economy would be in better condition if all Americans made a minimum of $50,000 before taxes: Thus, raise the minimum wage to $25.00 an hour. I truly wonder if all employees at Berkshire Hathaway Companies make a minimum of $50,000 yearly? Sounds like a great idea to me. **Of course, those at the top would have to take less**. I hear the conservative media pundits bemoan "Redistribution Of Income." But, I have not heard much complaint about the Redistribution Of Income from the poor and middle class to the top 20 percent over the last thirty years. (Thanks to Reganomics.)

Americans at the bottom of our wage scale must be helped immediately. The bottom twenty per cent of American workers by income – twenty eight million workers — earn less than $10.00 per hour. Recently, a company executive stated that remaining a stable employer requires remaining a financially strong company. I would say that remaining a financially strong employee requires being paid a decent living income. Companies who resort to part time employment to get out of paying a living wage and health care benefits should be ashamed of themselves. It would be better to have a reduction in the number of jobs at a particular company; at least those employees remaining will be adequately compensated with a Living Wage Income plus full benefits.

Many of America's largest companies (not, however, the greatest) have used ruthless strategies to hold down the cost of employee payroll: Part time employees who are paid less than full time employees for the same work; hiring temporary employees at less than a Living Wage Income to fill what were at one time full time positions; outright freezes on wage increases; and by not providing Company Health Insurance, forcing employees to sign up for Medicaid for personal and Family health insurance.

The Federal minimum wage was last raised in July 2009 to $7.25 per hour which equates to $15,080 annually. In 1968 the minimum wage was $1.60 per hour which adjusted for inflation is $10.75 in 2013, or $22,339 per year. This truth is shameful. Incomes increased by almost twenty percent in 2012 for the wealthiest top one percent. At the same time there was only a one percent increase in income for the other 99% of Americans.

At a time when Corporations are showing record profits and executives are being paid record salaries and bonuses, the American working man and woman is being robbed of his or her just due: A living wage income with full benefits. The President,

Congress, and ruthless, greedy Corporation Executives best learn how to treat people with more generous, American compensation plans. American working men and women – those who still have a job — have just about seen enough Corporate economic greed and selfishness to last two life times.

In 2012, CEO's of the largest US Companies made 354 times what the average worker was paid – the widest pay gap in the world. At 500 Standard and Poor Companies, CEO's received an average of $10.3 million dollars yearly (some say 15.1 million dollars) while rank and file workers took home around $35,000. In 1983, the disparity was just 42 times. Does anyone really wonder why America's once great Middle Class has been disappearing? Does the top twenty percent of our economic ladder realize the financial jeopardy in which all too many Americans exist? Does the top twenty per cent realize the bottom eighty percent will eventually react with anger and hostility, if an economic correction is not initiated. The top twenty percent must again learn what all too many have apparently forgotten: The United States Of America is a Republic, not an Oligarchy.

Recent economic data showed that the wealthiest top one percent in the United States earned more than 19% of the total household income in 2012 - - the biggest share of the income since 1928. Just as unfair, the wealthiest top 10% of United States Citizens earned over 48% of the total income in 2012.

While looking through papers, documents, and souvenirs of my past, my memory was refreshed of earlier times. I found some of my things wrapped in old newspapers. Lo and behold, I found in the *Portland Oregonian* — dated September 15, 1963 — the following letter to the editor:

Amazing isn't it, that the late Ms. Rice, a very intelligent woman of Tillamook, Oregon, sent a letter to our leaders in 1963 through the *Portland Oregonian* that, had those leaders followed her plea for common sense, could have saved the United States over fifty thousand beautiful American lives and a trillion dollars in taxpayers' money in the Vietnam War. (Let alone the death of hundreds of thousands of Vietnamese men, women, and children.)

Remember, the late Ms. Rice's letter was written over fifty years ago, just prior to President Kennedy's assassination, which some conspiracy theorists allege was in part caused by his position against the United States getting involved in Vietnam. In my mind, the greatest military leader who ever served as President of the United States of America was Supreme Allied Commander Five Star General of the Army Dwight D. Eisenhower. After consultation with his Budget Director about America rescuing the French in Vietnam, and learning the cost to American taxpayers would be over two billion dollars, without hesitation President Eisenhower **DENIED the French our Military's Blood and Country's Treasure.** NO questions asked; decision quickly and correctly made !!

Oregonian Readers Say . . .

Khrushchev And Tito Had Reason To Dance

To the Editor: We who have repeatedly rallied against continuation of foreign aid seem to be in position to say, "I told you so." At long last the House and Senate appear to be in revolt and if part of it is motivated by spiteful Southerners holding key committees the results should be balm to bleeding taxpayers' wounds. (Hurrah and Bravo! Southern senators, plus Proxmire and Mansfield, plus members of the Appropriations Committee.)

What more does it take, aside from our depleted gold reserves, to notify our federal government that we are going bankrupt? That we are not going to continue to support 96 foreign countries which include those far more prosperous than the U.S. and too many of them being Communist satellite countries.

How long will we listen to the State Department's defense of aid which says we must support Communist countries at the same time we are supposed to be fighting communism? How long can we tolerate an Administration that places every country's interest ahead of ours? What country is he president of, anyway?

France and Viet Nam deserve each other. If De Gaulle really wants to take on the running of that country it should be handed him at once. Any time President De Gaulle spends one million dollars a day in support of that country's freedom he will make sure it is to his country's benefit. Can the same be said of this country where suckers pay income tax for the privilege of supporting foreign dictators?

I should like to ask President Kennedy and his State Department if any member knows a country more in need of a Marshall Plan than the poor, old and staggering United States. Do they know any country nearer a revolt over high taxes and unemployment? Do they know why Khrushchev and Tito danced for joy in a Yugoslavian street? Was it over the test ban treaty or our imminent burial through national bankruptcy?

JEWELL ETHEL RICE,
2206 10th St.,
Tillamook.

*Printed with permission of Ms. Christine Hassing,
Great Granddaughter of Ms. Jewell Ethel Rice*

America must never forget what our Politicians and the so called "The Best and the Brightest" — some from such revered universities as Harvard, Princeton and Yale — did to their fellow Americans: Starting a totally unnecessary land war in Asia which cost the United States over 50,000 beautiful American lives and over a trillion dollars of Treasure. These Leaders should be called "The Worst and the Dumbest !" If these phony geniuses had ever read the history of the adversarial relationship between China and Viet Nam, the Domino Theory would have tumbled straight into the Potomac River. The lie of the attack on our ships in the Tonkin Gulf was only topped by the lie of the WMD in Iraq. Good Americans died and much Treasure was wasted after dishonorable American Leadership failed to tell Citizens the truth about why the United States was going to war, in both instances: American Political Hubris and The Lobby Power of the Industrial Military Complex. A great amount of family grief and heartache and badly needed National Revenue could have been saved if our Leaders had been more honorable men. I know some "Die Hards" will disagree with my observations, but I suspect many more will shout "Right On !"

The difference between the late Ms. Rice's time and now is our nation's almost twenty-billion-dollar national debt. Some very bright men and women say time is running out. Fellow Americans, either we stop foolishly wasting precious dollars (borrowed Chinese money) and start reducing our national debt or we will soon become a third-rate Country, unable to regain financial solvency.

Let's feed and clothe the world only AFTER we take care of our own starving and homeless here in the United States. I repeat, let's only go to War when *Our* Nation's Security is TRULY at stake. Let's get out of debt and remain that way! The interest on the national debt is a terrible waste of hard-earned US tax dollars.

Since World War II when the United States of America saved the world from totalitarianism, we have wasted trillions of dollars and thousands of beautiful American Lives on limited wars based on sheer politics. Our nation's real security was never at stake in any of these endeavors: Korea, Vietnam, Iraq, and Afghanistan. None of these countries were ever capable of invading the United States of America. The initial military response to the 9/11 attack on the United States was absolutely necessary and appropriate; the terrible waste of American Lives and Treasure over the last ten years was not. The United States is not good at nation building. We must admit it is impossible to make true friends or change closed minds at the point of a gun. Common sense tells us love will always conquer hate. We should only help those Countries who invite our help and are also willing to work hard to help themselves.

The Iraq War was a terrible, unnecessary and costly abomination. If former President George Bush and Vice President Dick Chaney had served one day in Viet Nam, I doubt if they would have ever invaded Iraq. The loss of a Trillion Dollars and over 4,000 Beautiful American Military lives is unforgivable; both men should hang their heads in shame. Look at Iraq now: The United States really made a difference, didn't we!

My Wife and I are thankful to God that we did not lose our US Army Chinook Helicopter Pilot Son during his two years of service in Iraq and one year in Afghanistan. Our love and prayers go out to those unfortunate American Families who did lose a loved one in this very avoidable and tragic war; and to those brave Military Men and Women who were tragically injured during the wars.

In my lifetime, the United States has been the most generous country in the world in providing Foreign Aid. When conflict ceased, we have invested billions of dollars to rebuild economies and ways of life in Europe, Korea, Vietnam, Iraq, and Afghanistan. We have helped our friends and adversaries alike rebuild their manufacturing plants. We have opened our markets to their products, chiefly duty free. To rebuild *our* way of life, now the time has come to put the United States citizens FIRST when our leaders make decisions to spend US tax dollars. The rest of the world must understand how dire our current financial situation is and the economic disaster forthcoming, if we do not act quickly. Our almost twenty-trillion dollar national debt, which is the single most important problem facing our nation, will destroy the United States as we know it, if a national debt-reduction program is not commenced immediately.

During much of the last fifty years, the United States has also invested trillions of dollars in fighting the Cold War with the Soviet Union. I respect our Government Officials and Military Leadership for the correct decisions they made. My prayers are with the Military Families whose loved ones were lost while fighting this war. The war is now over: the United States won. A Republic is better system of government than a communistic society. The reason is simple: People everywhere have an innate desire to be free. While the threat of nuclear warfare is still prevalent in the world, the two superpowers are now at peace with each other. I believe the whole world owes a debt of thanks to Madame Prime Minister Margaret Thatcher, President Ronald Reagan, and President Mikhail Gorbachev. We must thank God as well.

In 2008 my son Darrick, our Hollywood Handsome US Army Boeing Chinook Helicopter Instructor Pilot, returned home from a tour of duty in Afghanistan. Darrick and his son Tyler lived at home with his Mother and me for a short period. During this time, I had a Cardiac Arrest. Darrick saved my life by providing CPR immediately. Darrick said, "No Dad, Not I! God saved your life because you have more to accomplish before leaving us for good!" Perhaps finishing *"Rock Hill"* and *"America's Opportunities"* is part of my task. I pray these thoughts bring some wisdom to my fellow Americans and cause some to take action. I am the first to admit that none of us have all the answers to our Nation's current problems. All Americans must be challenged to provide solutions. Remember, in our Country, everyone is entitled to his opinion; objective criticism is the backbone of our American Way Of Life.

For over two hundred years we have operated our Government using Judeo-Christian Ethics and the United States Constitution. I see no reason why we should change. I believe in the goodness of the United States of America. I believe in the wholesomeness of our people. We need to work together with our leaders — the President, Congress, and the Judiciary — to take action to improve the lives of all our people. We can improve our Country by always adhering to the Constitution of the United States of America! I believe, with prayer, leadership, and a burning desire to succeed, we can and will add value to the lives of ALL Americans. Then, once we solve our problems here at home, the United States will be in a better position to help others around the world.

President Theodore Roosevelt said long ago not to criticize unless you are willing to get into the arena. I believe every US citizen, rich or poor, young or old, should take action politically to return the United States of America to its former place of greatness. We must act now! Let our leaders know we expect them to solve America's problems first and now. Let there be no misunderstanding**: I KNOW I do not have all of the answers to the problems of our Country. In fact, in the minds of many very smart and responsible people, I may have Few or even NONE. Unfortunately, many political and religious leaders think *They Alone Know Best.* All United States citizens must make their positions known through the ballot box on election day. We must all enter the arena to vote according to our beliefs; the economic and social condition of our Country today makes it mandatory why Citizens should not be impeded from their Constitutional Right To Register and To Vote their position.**

In the meantime, it is time for all Americans to stop just blaming the President, Members of the House and Senate or the Judiciary for the economic and social conditions of the United States. Remember, The US Government is composed of Citizens like you and me. Through the use of the ballot box, the party system (Progressives, Liberals, Centrists, Conservatives, and Independents, like me), blogs, and the massive power of social media, **Americans CAN, WILL, AND MUST right the American Ship Of State to again become an economically sound and more just country.**

Long ago, the famous newspaper cartoon character Pogo said, **"The enemy is us."** Together, we must NOW start building America's Future by solving our current problems.

In closing, I would point out to my fellow Americans that America's future may be one of living in a United States where Anglo people no longer dominate the United States economically, politically, socially, or just in numbers. In the United States melting pot where races usually mix without hostility, all Citizens should have nothing to worry about. Roll your sleeves up, go to work, and compete in the market place of America's Opportunities.

To be an informed citizen, I have always believed that one must read throughout life. My Father was a "Voracious" reader; I have tried to be. Neither one of us had a College Education. Because of the Great Depression, my Father never had a chance to finish High School or attend College; I chose to live a very active life, rather than finish College; and to tell you the truth, I am Not Sorry for that decision.

To all I would emphatically state: **Read, Read, Read! Ignorance is the Handiwork of the Lazy.**

Finally, I would ask my fellow Americans to always remember the positive impact Prayer can have on one's life. With God's help, there is NO problem The United States cannot solve!

When I was A young man, a wise Teacher said to me, "Jim
"America's Problems Are Opportunities Awaiting Solutions."

IN GOD WE TRUST

MANIFESTOES

To provide words for thought for my fellow Americans, I have selected famous speeches mostly in the public domain, primarily given by elected officials. **Five Star General Douglas MacArthur's *"Farewell Speech"* at West Point to the Cadets is first on the list to remind all Americans of the importance of Duty and Honor to Country by all Citizens to change the Political and Economic direction of the United States of America**. Remember: "The more things change, the more things remain the same," especially if the electorate allows Congress and the President to kowtow to rich citizens and corporations in this Country which according to the United States Constitution is supposed to be "Of the People, By the People, and for the People."

Some paragraphs of these Speeches have been highlighted in **bold print** to emphasize important comments about problems of yesterday that are either very important or very similar to our problems of today. Many of our Nation's challenges revolve around **pure greed** on the part of, **ONE**, International Corporations who maintain, though they are headquartered here, the United States is just one of their markets, **TWO**, the top 20 per cent of our population who own 89 per cent of our Country's private wealth and, **THREE,** Elected Officials who acquiesce to the power and lure of lobby money. A thorough reading will prove today's challenges are not new or unique in our Republic.

"There is nothing new in the world except the history you do not Know."

President Harry S. Truman

FIVE STAR GENERAL
DOUGLAS MacARTHUR

Born: January 26. 1880
Died: April 5, 1964

 FAREWELL SPEECH

GIVEN TO THE CORPS OF CADETS AT WEST POINT
May 12, 1962

General Westmoreland, General Groves, distinguished guests, and gentlemen of the Corps. As I was leaving the hotel this morning, a doorman asked me, "Where are you bound for, General?" and when I replied, "West Point," he remarked, "Beautiful place, have you ever been there before?"

No human being could fail to be deeply moved by such a tribute as this, coming from a profession I have served so long and a people I have loved so well. It fills me with an emotion I cannot express. But this award is not intended primarily for a personality, but to symbolize a great moral code - the code of conduct and chivalry of those who guard this beloved land of culture and ancient descent. That is the meaning of this medallion. For all eyes and for all time, it is an expression of the ethics of the American soldier. That I should be integrated in this way with so noble an ideal arouses a sense of pride and yet of humility which will be with me always.

Duty, Honor, Country: Those three hallowed words reverently dictate what you ought to be, what you can be, what you will be. They are your rallying points: to build courage when courage seems to fail; to regain faith when there seems to be little cause for faith; to create hope when hope becomes forlorn. Unhappily, I possess neither that eloquence of diction, that poetry of imagination, nor that brilliance of metaphor to tell you all that they mean.

The unbelievers will say they are but words, but a slogan, but a flamboyant phrase. Every pedant, every demagogue, every cynic, every hypocrite, every troublemaker, and, I am sorry to say, some others of an entirely different character, will try to downgrade them even to the extent of mockery and ridicule.

But these are some of the things they do. They build your basic character. They mold you for your future roles as the custodians of the nation's defense. They make you strong enough to know when you are weak, and brave enough to face yourself when you are afraid.

They teach you to be proud and unbending in honest failure, but humble and gentle in success; not to substitute words for action; not to seek the path of comfort, but to face the stress and spur of difficulty and challenge; to learn to stand up in the storm, but to have compassion on those who fall; to master yourself before you seek to master others; to have a heart that is clean, a goal that is high; to learn to laugh, yet never forget how to weep; to reach into the future, yet never neglect the past; to be serious, yet never take yourself too seriously; to be modest so that you will remember the simplicity of true greatness; the open mind of true wisdom, the meekness of true strength.

They give you a temperate will, a quality of imagination, a vigor of the emotions, a freshness of the deep springs of life, a temperamental predominance of courage over timidity, an appetite for adventure over love of ease. They create in your heart the sense of wonder, the unfailing hope of what next, and the joy and inspiration of life. They teach you in this way to be an officer and a gentleman.

And what sort of soldiers are those you are to lead? Are they reliable? Are they brave? Are they capable of victory?

Their story is known to all of you. It is the story of the American man at arms. My estimate of him was formed on the battlefields many, many years ago, and has never changed. I regarded him then, as I regard him now, as one of the world's noblest figures; not only as one of the finest military characters, but also as one of the most stainless.

His name and fame are the birthright of every American citizen. In his youth and strength, his love and loyalty, he gave all that mortality can give. He needs no eulogy from me, or from any other man. He has written his own history and written it in red on his enemy's breast.

But when I think of his patience under adversity, of his courage under fire, and of his modesty in victory, I am filled with an emotion of admiration I cannot put into words. He belongs to history as furnishing one of the greatest examples of successful patriotism. He belongs to posterity as the instructor of future generations in the principles of liberty and freedom. He belongs to the present, to us, by his virtues and by his achievements.

In twenty campaigns, on a hundred battlefields, around a thousand campfires, I have witnessed that enduring fortitude, that patriotic self-abnegation, and that invincible determination which have carved his statue in the hearts of his people.

From one end of the world to the other, he has drained deep the chalice of courage.

As I listened to those songs of the glee club, in memory's eye I could see those staggering columns of the First World War, bending under soggy packs on many a weary march, from dripping dusk to drizzling dawn, slogging ankle deep through mire of shell-pocked roads; to form grimly for the attack, blue-lipped, covered with sludge and mud, chilled by the wind and rain, driving home to their objective, and for many, to the judgment seat of God.

I do not know the dignity of their birth, but I do know the glory of their death. They died unquestioning, uncomplaining, with faith in their hearts, and on their lips the hope that we would go on to victory. Always for them: Duty, Honor, Country. Always their blood, and sweat, and tears, as they saw the way and the light.

And twenty years after, on the other side of the globe, against the filth of dirty foxholes, the stench of ghostly trenches, the slime of dripping dugouts, those boiling suns of the relentless heat, those torrential rains of devastating storms, the loneliness and utter desolation of jungle trails, the bitterness of long separation of those they loved and cherished, the deadly pestilence of tropic disease, the horror of stricken areas of war.

Their resolute and determined defense, their swift and sure attack, their indomitable purpose, their complete and decisive victory - always victory, always through the bloody haze of their last reverberating shot, the vision of gaunt, ghastly men, reverently following your password of Duty, Honor, Country.

The code which those words perpetuate embraces the highest moral laws and will stand the test of any ethics or philosophies ever promulgated for the uplift of mankind. Its requirements are for the things that are right, and its restraints are from the things that are wrong. The soldier, above all other men, is required to practice the greatest act of religious training - sacrifice. In battle and in the face of danger and death, he discloses those divine attributes which his Maker gave when he created man in his own image. No physical courage and no brute instinct can take the place of the Divine help which alone can sustain him. However horrible the incidents of war may be, the soldier who is called upon to offer and to give his life for his country, is the noblest development of mankind.

You now face a new world, a world of change. The thrust into outer space of the satellite, spheres and missiles marked the beginning of another epoch in the long story of mankind - the chapter of the space age. In the five or more billions of years the scientists tell us it has taken to form the earth, in the three or more billion years of development of the human race, there has never been a greater, a more abrupt or staggering evolution. We deal now not with things of this world alone, but with the illimitable distances and as yet unfathomed mysteries of the universe. We are reaching out for a new and boundless frontier. We speak in strange terms: of harnessing the cosmic energy; of making winds and tides work for us; of creating unheard synthetic materials to supplement or even replace our old standard basics; of purifying sea water for our drink; of mining ocean floors for new fields of wealth and food; of disease preventatives to expand life into the hundred of years; of controlling the weather for a more equitable distribution of heat and cold, of rain and shine; of space ships to the moon; of the primary target in war, no longer limited to the armed forces of an enemy, but instead to include his civil populations; of ultimate conflict between a united human race and the sinister forces of some other planetary galaxy; of such dreams and fantasies as to make life the most exciting of all time.

And through all this welter of change and development your mission remains fixed, determined, inviolable. It is to win our wars. Everything else in your professional career is but corollary to this vital dedication. All other public purpose, all other public projects, all other public needs, great or small, will find others for their accomplishments; but you are the ones who are trained to fight.

Yours is the profession of arms, the will to win, the sure knowledge that in war there is no substitute for victory, that if you lose, the Nation will be destroyed, that the very obsession of your public service must be Duty, Honor, Country.

Others will debate the controversial issues, national and international, which divide men's minds. But serene, calm, aloof, you stand as the Nation's war guardians, as its lifeguards from the raging tides of international conflict, as its gladiators in the arena of battle. For a century and a half you have defended, guarded and protected its hallowed traditions of liberty and freedom, of right and justice.

Let civilian voices argue the merits or demerits of our processes of government. Whether our strength is being sapped by deficit financing indulged in too long, by federal paternalism grown too mighty, by power groups grown too arrogant, by politics grown too corrupt, by crime grown too rampant, by morals grown too low, by taxes grown too high, by extremists grown too violent; whether our personal liberties are as firm and complete as they should be.

These great national problems are not for your professional participation or military solution. Your guidepost stands out like a tenfold beacon in the night: Duty, Honor, Country.

You are the leaven which binds together the entire fabric of our national system of defense. From your ranks come the great captains who hold the Nation's destiny in their hands the moment the war tocsin sounds.

The long gray line has never failed us. Were you to do so, a million ghosts in olive drab, in brown khaki, in blue and gray, would rise from their white crosses, thundering those magic words: Duty, Honor, Country.

This does not mean that you are warmongers. On the contrary, the soldier above all other people prays for peace, for he must suffer and bear the deepest wounds and scars of war. But always in our ears ring the ominous words of Plato, that wisest of all philosophers: "Only the dead have seen the end of war."

The shadows are lengthening for me. The twilight is here. My days of old have vanished - tone and tints. They have gone glimmering through the dreams of things that were. Their memory is one of wondrous beauty, watered by tears and coaxed and caressed by the smiles of yesterday.

I listen then, but with thirsty ear, for the witching melody of faint bugles blowing reveille, of far drums beating the long roll.

In my dreams I hear again the crash of guns, the rattle of musketry, the strange, mournful mutter of the battlefield. But in the evening of my memory I come back to West Point. Always there echoes and re-echoes: Duty, Honor, Country.

Today marks my final roll call with you. But I want you to know that when I cross the river, my last conscious thoughts will be of the Corps, and the Corps, and the Corps.

I bid you farewell.

RABBI JOACHIM PRINZ

Born: May 10, 1902
Died: September 30, 1988

A SPEECH GIVEN ON AUGUST 28, 1963 AT THE CIVIL RIGHTS MARCH ON WASHINGTON "SILENCE"

As Americans we share the profound concern of millions of people about the shame and disgrace of inequality and injustice which make a mockery of the great American idea.

As Jews we bring to this great demonstration, in which thousands of us proudly participate, a two-fold experience — one of the spirit and one of our history.

In the realm of the spirit, our fathers taught us thousands of years ago that when God created man, he created him as everybody's neighbor. Neighbor is not a geographic term. It is a moral concept. It means our collective responsibility for the preservation of man's dignity and integrity.

From our Jewish historic experience of three and a half thousand years we say:

Our ancient history began with slavery and the yearning for freedom. During the Middle Ages my people lived for a thousand years in the ghettos of Europe. Our modern history begins with a proclamation *of* emancipation.

It is for these reasons that it is not merely sympathy and compassion for the black people of America that motivates us. It is above all and beyond all such sympathies and emotions a sense of complete identification and solidarity born of our own painful historic experience.

When I was the rabbi of the Jewish community in Berlin under the Hitler regime, I learned many things. The most important thing that I learned under those tragic circumstances was that bigotry and hatred are not the most urgent problem. The most urgent, the most disgraceful, the most shameful and the most tragic problem is silence.

A great people which had created a great civilization had become a nation of silent onlookers. They remained silent in the face of hate, in the face of brutality and in the face of mass murder.

America must not become a nation of onlookers. America must not remain silent. Not merely black America , but all of America . It must speak up and act, from the President down to the humblest of us, and not for the sake of the Negro, not for the sake of the black community but for the sake of the image, the idea and the aspiration of America itself.

Our children, yours and mine in every school across the land, each morning pledge allegiance to the flag of the United States and to the republic for which it stands. They, the children, speak fervently and innocently of this land as the land of "liberty and justice for all."

The time, I believe, has come to work together - for it is not enough to hope together, and it is not enough to pray together, to work together that this children's oath, pronounced every morning from Maine to California, from North to South, may become. a glorious, unshakeable reality in a morally renewed and United America.

*** Used with the permission of The Prinz Family ***

US HOUSE OF REPRESENTATIVES
BARBARA LEE
CALIFORNIA, 13TH DISTRICT.

Born: July 16, 1946

SPEECH OPPOSING THE AUTHORIZATION FOR USE OF MILITARY FORCE AGAINST TERRORIST ACT

September 14, 2001

Mr. Speaker, I rise today with a heavy heart, one that is filled with sorrow for the families and loved ones who were killed and injured in New York, Virginia, and Pennsylvania. Only the most foolish or the most callous would not understand the grief that has gripped the American people and millions around the world.

This unspeakable attack on the United States has forced me to rely on my moral compass, my conscience, and my God for direction.

September 11 changed the world. Our deepest fears now haunt us. Yet I am convinced that military action will not prevent further acts of international terrorism against the United States.

I know that this use-of -force resolution will pass although we all know that the President can wage war even without this resolution. However difficult this vote may be, some of us must urge the use of restraint. There must be some of us who say, let's step back for a moment and think through the implications of our actions today-let us more fully understand their consequences.

We are not dealing with a conventional war. We cannot respond in a conventional manner. I do not want to see this spiral out of control. This crisis involves issues of national security, foreign policy, public safety, intelligence gathering, economics, and murder. Our response must be equally multifaceted.

We must not rush to judgment. For too many innocent people have already died. Our country is in mourning. If we rush to launch a counterattack, we run too great a risk that woman, children, and other non-combatants will be caught in the crossfire.

Nor can we let our justified anger over these outrageous acts by vicious murderers inflame prejudice against all Arab Americans, Muslim, Southeast Asians, and any other people because of their race, religion, or ethnicity.

Finally, we must be careful not to embark on an open-ended war with neither an exit strategy nor a focused target. We cannot repeat past mistakes.

In 1964, Congress gave President Lyndon Johnson the power to "take all necessary measures" to repel attacks and prevent further aggression. In so doing, this House abandoned its own constitutional responsibilities and launched our country into years of undeclared war in Vietnam.

At this time, Senator Wayne Morse, one of the two lonely votes against the Tonkin Gulf Resolution, declared, "I believe that history will record that we have made a grave mistake in subverting and circumventing the Constitution of the United States. I believe that with the next century, future generations will look with dismay and great disappointment upon a Congress which is now about to make such a historic mistake."

Senator Morse was correct, and I fear we make the same mistake today. And I fear the consequences. I have agonized over this vote. But I came to grips with it in the very painful yet beautiful memorial service today at the National Cathedral. As a member of the clergy so eloquently said, " As we act, let us not become the evil that we deplore.

# WHY I OPPOSED THE RESOLUTION TO AUTHORIZE FORCE

Published 4:00 am, Sunday, September 23, 2001

On Sept. 11, terrorists attacked the United States in an unprecedented and brutal manner, killing thousands of innocent people, including the passengers and crews of four aircraft.

Like everyone throughout our country, I am repulsed and angered by these attacks and believe all appropriate steps must be taken to bring the perpetrators to justice.

We must prevent any future such attacks. That is the highest obligation of our federal, state and local governments. On this, we are united as a nation. Any nation, group or individual that fails to comprehend this or believes that we will tolerate such illegal and uncivilized attacks is grossly mistaken.

Last week, filled with grief and sorrow for those killed and injured and with anger at those who had done this, I confronted the solemn responsibility of voting to authorize the nation to go to war. Some believe this resolution was only symbolic, designed to show national resolve. But I could not ignore that it provided explicit authority, under the War Powers Resolution and the Constitution, to go to war.

It was a blank check to the president to attack anyone involved in the Sept. 11 events — anywhere, in any country, without regard to our nation's long-term foreign policy, economic and national security interests, and without time limit. In granting these overly broad powers, the Congress failed its responsibility to understand the dimensions of its declaration. I could not support such a grant of war-making authority to the president; I believe it would put more innocent lives at risk.

The president has the constitutional authority to protect the nation from further attack and he has mobilized the armed forces to do just that. The Congress should have waited for the facts to be presented and then acted with fuller knowledge of the consequences of our action.

I have heard from thousands of my constituents in the wake of this vote. Many — a majority — have counseled restraint and caution, demanding that we ascertain the facts and ensure that violence does not beget violence. They understand the boundless consequences of proceeding hastily to war, and I thank them for their support.

Others believe that I should have voted for the resolution — either for symbolic or geopolitical reasons, or because they truly believe a military option is unavoidable. However, I am not convinced that voting for the resolution preserves and protects U.S. interests. We must develop our intelligence and bring those who did this to justice. We must mobilize and maintain an international coalition against terrorism. Finally, we have a chance to demonstrate to the world that great powers can choose to fight on the fronts of their choosing, and that we can choose to avoid needless military action when other avenues to redress our rightful grievances and to protect our nation are available to us.

We must respond, but the character of that response will determine for us and for our children the world that they will inherit. I do not dispute the president's intent to rid the world of terrorism — but we have many means to reach that goal, and measures that spawn further acts of terror or that do not address the sources of hatred do not increase our security.

Secretary of State Colin Powell himself eloquently pointed out the many ways to get at the root of this problem — economic, diplomatic, legal and political, as well as military. A rush to launch precipitous military counterattacks runs too great a risk that more innocent men, women, children will be killed. I could not vote for a resolution that I believe could lead to such an outcome.

Final U.S. House Vote:
FOR: 420
AGAINST: 1 (Congresswoman Barbara Lee)

Leave it to an Articulate, Beautiful, Distinguished, Intelligent Woman to exhibit a true Profile In Courage ! J.A.N

Few men are willing to brave the disapproval of their fellows, the censure of their colleagues, the wrath of their society. Moral courage is a rarer commodity than bravery in battle or great intelligence. Yet it is the one essential, vital quality of those who seek to change a world which yields most painfully to change.

- U.S. Senator Robert F. Kennedy (1925 - 1968)

US SENATOR
ROBERT C. BYRD
WEST VIRGINIA

Born: November 20, 1917
Died: June 28, 2010

Senate Floor Speech — Wednesday, February 12, 2003

"SLEEPWALKING THROUGH HISTORY"

To contemplate war is to think about the most horrible of human experiences. On this February day, as this nation stands at the brink of battle, every American on some level must be contemplating the horrors of war.

Yet, this Chamber is, for the most part, silent — ominously, dreadfully silent. There is no debate, no discussion, no attempt to lay out for the nation the pros and cons of this particular war. There is nothing.

We stand passively mute in the United States Senate, paralyzed by our own uncertainty, seemingly stunned by the sheer turmoil of events. Only on the editorial pages of our newspapers is there much substantive discussion of the prudence or imprudence of engaging in this particular war.

And this is no small conflagration we contemplate. This is no simple attempt to defang a villain. No. This coming battle, if it materializes, represents a turning point in U.S. foreign policy and possibly a turning point in the recent history of the world.

This nation is about to embark upon the first test of a revolutionary doctrine applied in an extraordinary way at an unfortunate time. The doctrine of preemption — the idea that the United States or any other nation can legitimately attack a nation that is not imminently threatening but may be threatening in the future — is a radical new twist on the traditional idea of self defense. It appears to be in contravention of international law and the UN Charter. And it is being tested at a time of world-wide terrorism, making many countries around the globe wonder if they will soon be on our — or some other nation's — hit list. High level Administration figures recently refused to take nuclear weapons off of the table when discussing a possible attack against Iraq. What could be more destabilizing and unwise than this type of uncertainty, particularly in a world where globalism has tied the vital economic and security interests of

many nations so closely together? There are huge cracks emerging in our time-honored alliances, and U.S. intentions are suddenly subject to damaging worldwide speculation. Anti-Americanism based on mistrust, misinformation, suspicion, and alarming rhetoric from U.S. leaders is fracturing the once solid alliance against global terrorism which existed after September 11.

Here at home, people are warned of imminent terrorist attacks with little guidance as to when or where such attacks might occur. Family members are being called to active military duty, with no idea of the duration of their stay or what horrors they may face. Communities are being left with less than adequate police and fire protection. Other essential services are also short-staffed. The mood of the nation is grim. The economy is stumbling. Fuel prices are rising and may soon spike higher.

This Administration, now in power for a little over two years, must be judged on its record. I believe that that record is dismal.

In that scant two years, this Administration has squandered a large projected surplus of some $5.6 trillion over the next decade and taken us to projected deficits as far as the eye can see. This Administration's domestic policy has put many of our states in dire financial condition, under funding scores of essential programs for our people. This Administration has fostered policies which have slowed economic growth. This Administration has ignored urgent matters such as the crisis in health care for our elderly. This Administration has been slow to provide adequate funding for homeland security. This Administration has been reluctant to better protect our long and porous borders.

In foreign policy, this Administration has failed to find Osama bin Laden. In fact, just yesterday we heard from him again marshaling his forces and urging them to kill. This Administration has split traditional alliances, possibly crippling, for all time, International order-keeping entities like the United Nations and NATO. This Administration has called into question the traditional worldwide perception of the United States as well-intentioned, peacekeeper. This Administration has turned the patient art of diplomacy into threats, labeling, and name calling of the sort that reflects quite poorly on the intelligence and sensitivity of our leaders, and which will have consequences for years to come.

Calling heads of state pygmies, labeling whole countries as evil, denigrating powerful European allies as irrelevant — these types of crude insensitivities can do our great nation no good. We may have massive military might, but we cannot fight a global war on terrorism alone. We need the cooperation and friendship of our time-honored allies as well as the newer found friends whom we can attract with our wealth. Our awesome military machine will do us little good if we suffer another devastating attack on our homeland which severely damages our economy. Our military manpower is already stretched thin and we will need the augmenting support of those nations who can supply troop strength, not just sign letters cheering us on.

The war in Afghanistan has cost us $37 billion so far, yet there is evidence that terrorism may already be starting to regain its hold in that region. We have not found bin Laden, and unless we secure the peace in Afghanistan, the dark dens of terrorism may yet again flourish in that remote and devastated land.

Pakistan as well is at risk of destabilizing forces. This Administration has not finished the first war against terrorism and yet it is eager to embark on another conflict with perils much greater than those in Afghanistan. Is our attention span that short? Have we not learned that after winning the war one must always secure the peace?

And yet we hear little about the aftermath of war in Iraq. In the absence of plans, speculation abroad is rife. Will we seize Iraq's oil fields, becoming an occupying power which controls the price and supply of that nation's oil for the foreseeable future? To whom do we propose to hand the reigns of power after Saddam Hussein?

Will our war inflame the Muslim world resulting in devastating attacks on Israel? Will Israel retaliate with its own nuclear arsenal? Will the Jordanian and Saudi

Arabian governments be toppled by radicals, bolstered by Iran which has much closer ties to terrorism than Iraq?

Could a disruption of the world's oil supply lead to a world-wide recession? Has our senselessly bellicose language and our callous disregard of the interests and opinions of other nations increased the global race to join the nuclear club and made proliferation an even more lucrative practice for nations which need the income?

In only the space of two short years this reckless and arrogant Administration has initiated policies which may reap disastrous consequences for years.

One can understand the anger and shock of any President after the savage attacks of September 11. One can appreciate the frustration of having only a shadow to chase and an amorphous, fleeting enemy on which it is nearly impossible to exact retribution.

But to turn one's frustration and anger into the kind of extremely destabilizing and dangerous foreign policy debacle that the world is currently witnessing is inexcusable from any Administration charged with the awesome power and responsibility of guiding the destiny of the greatest superpower on the planet. Frankly many of the pronouncements made by this Administration are outrageous. There is no other word.

Yet this chamber is hauntingly silent. On what is possibly the eve of horrific infliction of death and destruction on the population of the nation of Iraq — a population, I might add, of which over 50% is under age 15 — this chamber is silent. On what is possibly only days before we send thousands of our own citizens to face unimagined horrors of chemical and biological warfare — this chamber is silent. On the eve of what could possibly be a vicious terrorist attack in retaliation for our attack on Iraq, it is business as usual in the United States Senate.

We are truly "sleepwalking through history." In my heart of hearts I pray that this great nation and its good and trusting citizens are not in for a rudest of awakenings.

To engage in war is always to pick a wild card. And war must always be a last resort, not a first choice. I truly must question the judgment of any President who can say that a massive unprovoked military attack on a nation which is over 50% children is "in the highest moral traditions of our country". This war is not necessary at this time. Pressure appears to be having a good result in Iraq. Our mistake was to put ourselves in a corner so quickly. Our challenge is to now find a graceful way out of a box of our own making. Perhaps there is still a way if we allow more time.

PRESIDENT ABRAHAM LINCOLN

Born: February 12, 1809
Assassinated: April 15, 1865

A HOUSE DIVIDED SPEECH

At Springfield, Illinois on June 16, 1858

Excerpts From Speech:

Mr. President and Gentlemen of the Convention: If we could first know where we are, and whither we are tending, we could better judge what to do, and how to do it. We are now far into the fifth year since a policy was initiated with the avowed object, and confident promise, of putting an end to slavery agitation. Under the operation of that policy, that agitation has not only not ceased, but has constantly augmented. In my opinion, it will not cease, until a crisis shall have been reached and passed. "A house divided against itself cannot stand." I believe this government cannot endure permanently half slave and half free. I do not expect the Union to be dissolved—I do not expect the house to fall—but I do expect it will cease to be divided. It will become all one thing, or all the other. Either the opponents of slavery will arrest the further spread of it, and place it where the public mind shall rest in the belief that it is in the course of ultimate extinction; or its advocates will push it forward, till it shall become alike lawful in all the States, old as well as new—North as well as South.

 # THANKSGIVING PROCLAMATION

October 3, 1863

The Year that is drawing to a close, has been filled with the blessings of fruitful fields and healthful skies. To these bounties, which are so constantly enjoyed that we are prone to forget the source from which they come, others have been added, which are so extraordinary a nature, that they cannot fail to penetrate and soften even the heart which is habitually insensible to the ever watchful providence of Almighty God.

In the midst of a civil war of unequaled magnitude and severity, which has sometimes seemed to foreign States to invite and to provoke the aggression, peace has been preserved with all nations, order has been maintained, the laws have been respected and obeyed, and harmony has prevailed everywhere except in the theater of military conflict; while that theater has been greatly contracted by the advancing armies and navies of the Union.

Needful diversion of wealth and strength from the fields of peaceful industry to the national defense, have not arrested the plough, the shuttle or the ship; the axe has enlarged the borders of our settlements, and the mines, as well of iron and coal as of the precious metals, have yielded even more abundantly than heretofore.

Population has steadily increased, notwithstanding the waste that has been made in the camp, the siege, and the battle-field; and the country, rejoicing in the consciousness of augmented strength and vigor, is permitted to expect continuance of years with large increase of freedom.

No human counsel hath devised nor hath any mortal hand worked out these great things. They are the gracious gifts of the Most High God, who, while dealing with us in anger for our sins, hath nevertheless remembered mercy.

It has seemed to me fit and proper that they should be solemnly, reverently and gratefully acknowledged as with one heart and one voice by the whole American People.

I do therefore invite my fellow citizens in every part of the United States, and also those who are at sea and those who are sojourning in foreign lands, to set apart and observe the last Thursday of November next, as a day of Thanksgiving and Praise to our beneficent Father who dwelleth in the Heavens.

And I recommend to them that while offering up the ascription's justly due to Him for such singular deliverance's and blessings, they do also, with humble penitence for our national perverseness and disobedience, commend to His tender care all those who have become widows, orphans, mourners or sufferers in the lamentable civil strife in which we are unavoidably engaged, and fervently implore the interposition of the Almighty hand to heal the wounds of the nation, and to restore it as soon as may be consistent with the Divine purposes to the full enjoyment of peace, harmony, tranquility, and Union.

In testimony whereof, I have hereunto set my hand and caused the seal of the United States to be affixed.

Done at the City of Washington, this Third day of October, in the year of our Lord one thousand eight hundred and sixty-three, and of the Independence of the United States the Eighty-eighth.

By the President: Abraham Lincoln

GETTYSBURG ADDRESS

November 19, 1863

Four score and seven years ago our fathers brought forth on this continent a new nation, conceived in liberty, and dedicated to the proposition that all men are created equal.

Now we are engaged in a great civil war, testing whether that nation, or any nation so conceived and so dedicated, can long endure. We are met on a great battlefield of that war. We have come to dedicate a portion of that field, as a final resting place for those who here gave their lives that that nation might live. It is altogether fitting and proper that we should do this.

But, in a larger sense, we can not dedicate, we can not consecrate, we can not hallow this ground. The brave men, living and dead, who struggled here, have consecrated it, far above our poor power to add or detract. The world will little note, nor long remember what we say here, but it can never forget what they did here. It is for us the living, rather, to be dedicated here to the unfinished work which they who fought here have thus far so nobly advanced. It is rather for us to be here dedicated to the great task remaining before us—that from these honored dead we take increased devotion to that cause for which they gave the last full measure of devotion—that we here highly resolve that these dead shall not have died in vain—that this nation, under God, shall have a new birth of freedom—and that government of the people, by the people, for the people, shall not perish from the earth.

 # SECOND INAUGURAL ADDRESS

March 4, 1865

Fellow-Countrymen:

AT this second appearing to take the oath of the Presidential office there is less occasion for an extended address than there was at the first. Then a statement somewhat in detail of a course to be pursued seemed fitting and proper. Now, at the expiration of four years, during which public declarations have been constantly called forth on every point and phase of the great contest which still absorbs the attention and engrosses the energies of the nation, little that is new could be presented. The progress of our arms, upon which all else chiefly depends, is as well known to the public as to myself, and it is, I trust, reasonably satisfactory and encouraging to all. With high hope for the future, no prediction in regard to it is ventured.

On the occasion corresponding to this four years ago all thoughts were anxiously directed to an impending civil war. All dreaded it, all sought to avert it. While the inaugural address was being delivered from this place, devoted altogether to saving the Union without war, insurgent agents were in the city seeking to destroy it without war—seeking to dissolve the Union and divide effects by negotiation. Both parties deprecated war, but one of them would make war rather than let the nation survive, and the other would accept war rather than let it perish, and the war came.

One-eighth of the whole population were colored slaves, not distributed generally over the Union, but localized in the southern part of it. These slaves constituted a peculiar and powerful interest. All knew that this interest was somehow the cause of the war. To strengthen, perpetuate, and extend this interest was the object for which the insurgents would rend the Union even by war, while the Government claimed no right to do more than to restrict the territorial enlargement of it. Neither party expected for the war the magnitude or the duration which it has already attained. Neither anticipated that the cause of the conflict might cease with or even before the conflict itself should cease. Each looked for an easier triumph, and a result less fundamental and astounding. Both read the same Bible and pray to the same God, and each invokes His aid against the other. It may seem strange that any men should dare to ask a just God's assistance in wringing their bread from the sweat of other men's faces, but let us judge not, that we be not judged. The prayers of both could not be answered. That of neither has been answered fully.

The Almighty has His own purposes. "Woe unto the world because of offenses; for it must needs be that offenses come, but woe to that man by whom the offense cometh." If we shall suppose that American slavery is one of those offenses which, in the providence of God, must needs come, but which, having continued through His appointed time, He now wills to remove, and that He gives to both North and

South this terrible war as the woe due to those by whom the offense came, shall we discern therein any departure from those divine attributes which the believers in a living God always ascribe to Him?

Fondly do we hope, fervently do we pray, that this mighty scourge of war may speedily pass away. Yet, if God wills that it continue until all the wealth piled by the bondsman's two hundred and fifty years of unrequited toil shall be sunk, and until every drop of blood drawn with the lash shall be paid by another drawn with the sword, as was said three thousand years ago, so still it must be said "the judgments of the Lord are true and righteous altogether."

With malice toward none, with charity for all, with firmness in the right as God gives us to see the right, let us strive on to finish the work we are in, to bind up the nation's wounds, to care for him who shall have borne the battle and for his widow and his orphan, to do all which may achieve and cherish a just and lasting peace among ourselves and with all nations.

PRESIDENT
THEODORE ROOSEVELT

Born: October 27, 1858
Died: January 6, 1919

"THE NEW NATIONALISM" SPEECH

Given on August 31, 1910, at Osawatomie, Kansas before a group of Civil War Veterans

Excerpts From Speech:

Of that generation of men to whom we owe so much, the man to whom we owe most is, of course, Lincoln. Part of our debt to him is because he forecast our present struggle and saw the way out.

Lincoln took substantially the attitude that we ought to take; he showed the proper sense of proportion in his relative estimates of capital and labor, of human rights and property rights. He taught a lesson in wise kindliness and charity; an indispensable lesson to us of today. But this wise kindliness and charity never weakened his arm or numbed his heart. We cannot afford weakly to blind ourselves to the actual conflict which faces us today. The issue is joined, and we must fight or fail.

In every wise struggle for human betterment one of the main objects, and often the only object, has been to achieve in large measure equality of opportunity. In the struggle for this great end, nations rise from barbarism to civilization, and through it people press forward from one stage of enlightenment to the next. One of the chief factors in progress is the destruction of special privilege. The essence of any struggle for healthy liberty has always been, and must always be, to take from some one man or class of men the right to enjoy power, or wealth, or position, or immunity, which has not been earned by service to his or their fellows. That is what you fought for in the Civil War, and that is what we strive for now.

At many stages in the advance of humanity, this conflict between the men who possess more than they have earned and the men who have earned more than they possess is the central condition of progress. In our day it appears as the struggle of freemen to gain and hold the right of self-government as against the special interests, who

twist the methods of free government into machinery for defeating the popular will. At every stage, and under all circumstances, the essence of the struggle is to equalize opportunity, destroy privilege, and give to the life and citizenship of every individual the highest possible value both to himself and to the commonwealth. That is nothing new.

All I ask in civil life is what you fought for in the Civil War. I ask that civil life be carried on according to the spirit in which the army was carried on. You never get perfect justice, but the effort in handling the army was to bring to the front the men who could do the job. Nobody grudged promotion to Grant, or Sherman, or Thomas, or Sheridan, because they earned it. The only complaint was when a man got promotion which he did not earn.

Practical equality of opportunity for all citizens, when we achieve it, will have two great results. First, every man will have a fair chance to make of himself all that in him lies; to reach the highest point to which his capacities, unassisted by special privilege of his own and unhampered by the special privilege of others, can carry him, and to get for himself and his family substantially what he has earned. Second, equality of opportunity means that the commonwealth will get from every citizen the highest service of which he is capable. No man who carries the burden of the special privileges of another can give to the commonwealth that service to which it is fairly entitled.

I stand for the square deal. But when I say that I am for the square deal, I mean not merely that I stand for fair play under the present rules of the game, but that I stand for having those rules changed so as to work for a more substantial equality of opportunity and of reward for equally good service. One word of warning, which, I think, is hardly necessary in Kansas. When I say I want a square deal for the poor man, I do not mean that I want a square deal for the man who remains poor because he has not got the energy to work for himself. If a man who has had a chance will not make good, then he has got to quit. And you men of the Grand Army, you want justice for the brave man who fought, and punishment for the coward who shirked his work. Is that not so?

Now, this means that our government, National and State, must be freed from the sinister influence or control of special interests. Exactly as the special interests of cotton and slavery threatened our political integrity before the Civil War, so now the great special business interests too often control and corrupt the men and methods of government for their own profit. We must drive the special interests out of politics. That is one of our tasks to-day.

Every special interest is entitled to justice—full, fair, and complete—and, now, mind you, if there were any attempt by mob-violence to plunder and work harm to the special interest, whatever it may be, that I most dislike, and the wealthy man, whomsoever he may be, for whom I have the greatest contempt, I would fight for him, and you would if you were worth your salt. He should have justice. For every special interest is entitled to justice, but not one is entitled to a vote in Congress, to a voice on the bench, or to representation in any public office. The Constitution guarantees protection to property, and we must make that promise good. But it does not give the right of suffrage to any corporation.

The true friend of property, the true conservative, is he who insists that property shall be the servant and not the master of the commonwealth; who insists that the creature of man's making shall be the servant and not the master of the man who made it. The citizens of the United States must effectively control the mighty commercial forces which they have called into being.

There can be no effective control of corporations while their political activity remains. To put an end to it will be neither a short nor an easy task, but it can be done.

We must have complete and effective publicity of corporate affairs, so that the people may know beyond peradventure whether the corporations obey the law and whether their management entitles them to the confidence of the public. It is necessary that laws should be passed to prohibit the use of corporate funds directly or indirectly for political purposes; it is still more necessary that such laws should be thoroughly enforced. Corporate expenditures for political purposes, and especially such expenditures by public-service corporations, have supplied one of the principal sources of corruption in our political affairs.

I believe that the officers, and, especially, the directors, of corporations should be held personally responsible when any corporation breaks the law.

PRESIDENT HERBERT HOOVER

Born: August 10, 1874
Died: October 20, 1964

INAUGURAL ADDRESS

Washington DC
March 4, 1929

Chief Justice William Howard Taft administered the oath on the East Portico of the Capitol.

My Countrymen

This occasion is not alone the administration of the most sacred oath which can be assumed by an American citizen. It is a dedication and consecration under God to the highest office in service of our people. I assume this trust in the humility of knowledge that only through the guidance of Almighty

Providence can I hope to discharge its ever-increasing burdens.

It is in keeping with tradition throughout our history that I should express simply and directly the opinions which I hold concerning some of the matters of present importance.

Our Progress

If we survey the situation of our Nation both at home and abroad, we find many satisfactions; we find some causes for concern. We have emerged from the losses of the Great War and the reconstruction following it with increased virility and strength. From this strength we have contributed to the recovery and progress of the world. What America has done has given renewed hope and courage to all who have faith in government by the people. In the large view, we have reached a higher degree of comfort and security than ever existed before in the history of the world. Through liberation from widespread poverty we have reached a higher degree of individual freedom than ever before. The devotion to and concern for our institutions are deep and sincere. We are steadily building a new race--a new civilization great in its own attainments. The influence and high purposes of our Nation are respected among the peoples of the world. We aspire to distinction in the world, but to a distinction based upon confidence in our sense of justice as well as our accomplishments within our own borders and in our own lives. For wise guidance in this great period of recovery the Nation is deeply indebted to Calvin Coolidge.

But all this majestic advance should not obscure the constant dangers from which self-government must be safeguarded. The strong man must at all times be alert to the attack of insidious disease.

The Failure of Our System of Criminal Justice

The most malign of all these dangers today is disregard and disobedience of law. Crime is increasing. Confidence in rigid and speedy justice is decreasing. I am not prepared to believe that this indicates any decay in the moral fiber of the American people. I am not prepared to believe that it indicates an impotence of the Federal Government to enforce its laws.

It is only in part due to the additional burdens imposed upon our judicial system by the eighteenth amendment. The problem is much wider than that. Many influences had increasingly complicated and weakened our law enforcement organization long before the adoption of the eighteenth amendment.

To reestablish the vigor and effectiveness of law enforcement we must critically consider the entire Federal machinery of justice, the redistribution of its functions, the simplification of its procedure, the provision of additional special tribunals, the better selection of juries, and the more effective organization of our agencies of investigation and prosecution that justice may be sure and that it may be swift. While the authority of the Federal Government extends to but part of our vast system of national, State, and local justice, yet the standards which the Federal Government establishes have the most profound influence upon the whole structure.

We are fortunate in the ability and integrity of our Federal judges and attorneys. But the system which these officers are called upon to administer is in many respects ill adapted to present-day conditions. Its intricate and involved rules of procedure have become the refuge of both big and little criminals. There is a belief abroad that by invoking technicalities, subterfuge, and delay, the ends of justice may be thwarted by those who can pay the cost.

Reform, reorganization and strengthening of our whole judicial and enforcement system, both in civil and criminal sides, have been advocated for years by statesmen, judges, and bar associations. First steps toward that end should not longer be delayed. Rigid and expeditious justice is the first safeguard of freedom, the basis of all ordered liberty, the vital force of progress. It must not come to be in our Republic that it can be defeated by the indifference of the citizen, by exploitation of the delays and entanglements of the law, or by combinations of criminals. Justice must not fail because the agencies of enforcement are either delinquent or inefficiently organized. To consider these evils, to find their remedy, is the most sore necessity of our times.

Enforcement of the 18th Amendment

Of the undoubted abuses which have grown up under the eighteenth amendment, part are due to the causes I have just mentioned; but part are due to the failure of some States to accept their share of responsibility for concurrent enforcement and to the failure of many State and local officials to accept the obligation under their oath of office zealously to enforce the laws. With the failures from these many causes has come a dangerous expansion in the criminal elements who have found enlarged opportunities in dealing in illegal liquor.

But a large responsibility rests directly upon our citizens. There would be little traffic in illegal liquor if only criminals patronized it. We must awake to the fact that this patronage from large numbers of law-abiding citizens is supplying the rewards and stimulating crime.

I have been selected by you to execute and enforce the laws of the country. I propose to do so to the extent of my own abilities, but the measure of success that the Government shall attain will depend upon the moral support which you, as citizens, extend. The duty of citizens to support the laws of the land is coequal with the duty of their Government to enforce the laws which exist. No greater national service can be given by men and women of good will--who, I know, are not unmindful of the responsibilities of citizenship--than that they should, by their example, assist in stamping out crime and outlawry by refusing participation in and condemning all transactions with illegal liquor. Our whole system of self-government will crumble either if officials elect what laws they will enforce or citizens elect what laws they will support. The worst evil of disregard for some law is that it destroys respect for all law. For our citizens to patronize the violation of a particular law on the ground that they are opposed to it is destructive of the very basis of all that protection of life, of homes and property which they rightly claim under other laws. If citizens do not like a law, their duty as honest men and women is to discourage its violation; their right is openly to work for its repeal.

To those of criminal mind there can be no appeal but vigorous enforcement of the law. Fortunately they are but a small percentage of our people. Their activities must be stopped.

A National Investigation

I propose to appoint a national commission for a searching investigation of the whole structure of our Federal system of jurisprudence, to include the method of enforcement of the eighteenth amendment and the causes of abuse under it. Its purpose will be to make such recommendations for reorganization of the administration of Federal laws and court procedure as may be found desirable. In the meantime it is essential that a large part of the enforcement activities be transferred from the Treasury Department to the Department of Justice as a beginning of more effective organization.

The Relation of Government to Business

The election has again confirmed the determination of the American people that regulation of private enterprise and not Government ownership or operation is the course rightly to be pursued in our relation to business. In recent years we have established a differentiation in the whole method of business regulation between the industries which produce and distribute commodities on the one hand and public utilities on the other. In the former, our laws insist upon effective competition; in the latter, because we substantially confer a monopoly by limiting competition, we must regulate their services and rates. The rigid enforcement of the laws applicable to both groups is the very base of equal opportunity and freedom from domination for all our people, and it is just as essential for the stability and prosperity of business itself as for the protection of the public at large. Such regulation should be extended by the Federal Government within the limitations of the Constitution and only when the individual States are without power to protect their citizens through their own authority. On the other hand, we should be fearless when the authority rests only in the Federal Government.

Cooperation by the Government

The larger purpose of our economic thought should be to establish more firmly stability and security of business and employment and thereby remove poverty still further from our borders. Our people have in recent years developed a new-found capacity for cooperation among themselves to effect high purposes in public welfare. It is an advance toward the highest conception of self-government. Self-government does not and should not imply the use of political agencies alone. Progress is born of cooperation in the community--not from governmental restraints. The Government should assist and encourage these movements of collective self- help by itself cooperating with them. Business has by cooperation made great progress in the advancement of service, in stability, in regularity of employment and in the correction of its own abuses. Such progress, however, can continue only so long as business manifests its respect for law.

There is an equally important field of cooperation by the Federal Government with the multitude of agencies, State, municipal and private, in the systematic development of those processes which directly affect public health, recreation, education, and the home. We have need further to perfect the means by which Government can be adapted to human service.

Education

Although education is primarily a responsibility of the States and local communities, and rightly so, yet the Nation as a whole is vitally concerned in its development everywhere to the highest standards and to complete universality. Self-government can succeed only through an instructed electorate. Our objective is not simply to overcome illiteracy. The Nation has Marched far beyond that. The more complex the problems of the Nation become, the greater is the need for more and more advanced instruction. Moreover, as our numbers increase and as our life expands with science and invention, we must discover more and more leaders for every walk of life. We can not hope to succeed in directing this increasingly complex civilization unless we can draw all the talent of leadership from the whole people. One civilization after another has been wrecked upon the attempt to secure sufficient leadership from a single group or class. If we would prevent the growth of class distinctions and would constantly refresh our leadership with the ideals of our people, we must draw constantly from the general mass. The full opportunity for every boy and girl to rise through the selective processes of education can alone secure to us this leadership.

Public Health

In public health the discoveries of science have opened a new era. Many sections of our country and many groups of our citizens suffer from diseases the eradication of which are mere matters of administration and moderate expenditure. Public health service should be as fully organized and as universally incorporated into our governmental system as is public education. The returns are a thousand fold in economic benefits, and infinitely more in reduction of suffering and promotion of human happiness.

World Peace

The United States fully accepts the profound truth that our own progress, prosperity, and peace are interlocked with the progress, prosperity, and peace of all humanity. The whole world is at peace. The dangers to a continuation of this peace to-day are largely the fear and suspicion which still haunt the world. No suspicion or fear can be rightly directed toward our country.

Those who have a true understanding of America know that we have no desire for territorial expansion, for economic or other domination of other peoples. Such purposes are repugnant to our ideals of human freedom. Our form of government is ill adapted to the responsibilities which inevitably follow permanent limitation of the independence of other peoples. Superficial observers seem to find no destiny for our abounding increase in population, in wealth and power except that of imperialism. They fail to see that the American people are engrossed in the building for themselves of a new economic system, a new social system, a new political system all of which are characterized by aspirations of freedom of opportunity and thereby are the negation of imperialism. They fail to realize that because of our abounding prosperity our youth are pressing more and more into our institutions of learning; that our people are seeking a larger vision through art, literature, science, and travel; that they are moving toward stronger moral and spiritual life--that from these things our sympathies are broadening beyond the bounds of our Nation and race toward their true expression in a real brotherhood of man. They fail to see that the idealism of America will lead it to no narrow or selfish channel, but inspire it to do its full share as a nation toward the advancement of civilization. It will do that not by mere declaration but by taking a practical part in supporting all useful international undertakings. We not only desire peace with the world, but to see peace maintained throughout the world. We wish to advance the reign of justice and reason toward the extinction of force.

The recent treaty for the renunciation of war as an instrument of national policy sets an advanced standard in our conception of the relations of nations. Its acceptance should pave the way to greater limitation of armament, the offer of which we sincerely extend to the world. But its full realization also implies a greater and greater perfection in the instrumentalities for pacific settlement of controversies between nations. In the creation and use of these instrumentalities we should support every sound method of conciliation, arbitration, and judicial settlement. American statesmen were among the first to propose and they have constantly urged upon the world, the establishment of a tribunal for the settlement of controversies of a justiciable character. The Permanent Court of International Justice in its major purpose is thus peculiarly identified with American ideals and with American statesmanship. No more potent instrumentality for this purpose has ever been conceived and no other is practicable of establishment. The reservations placed upon our adherence should not be misinterpreted. The United States seeks by these reservations no special privilege or advantage but only to clarify our relation to advisory opinions and other matters which are subsidiary to the major purpose of the court. The way should, and I believe will, be found by which we may take our proper place in a movement so fundamental to the progress of peace.

Our people have determined that we should make no political engagements such as membership in the League of Nations, which may commit us in advance as a nation to become involved in the settlements of controversies between other countries. They adhere to the belief that the independence of America from such obligations increases its ability and availability for service in all fields of human progress.

I have lately returned from a journey among our sister Republics of the Western Hemisphere. I have received unbounded hospitality and courtesy as their expression of friendliness to our country. We are held by particular bonds of sympathy and common interest with them. They are each of them building a racial character and a culture which is an impressive contribution to human progress. We wish only for the maintenance of their independence, the growth of their stability, and their prosperity. While we have had wars in the Western Hemisphere, yet on the whole the record is in encouraging contrast with that of other parts of the world. Fortunately the New World is largely free from the inheritances of fear and distrust which have so troubled the Old World. We should keep it so.

It is impossible, my countrymen, to speak of peace without profound emotion. In thousands of homes in America, in millions of homes around the world, there are vacant chairs. It would be a shameful confession of our unworthiness if it should develop that we have abandoned the hope for which all these men died. Surely civilization is old enough, surely mankind is mature enough so that we ought in our own lifetime to find a way to permanent peace. Abroad, to west and east, are nations whose sons mingled their blood with the blood of our sons on the battlefields. Most of these nations have contributed to our race, to our culture, our knowledge, and our progress. From one of them we derive our very language and from many of them much of the genius of our institutions. Their desire for peace is as deep and sincere as our own.

Peace can be contributed to by respect for our ability in defense. Peace can be promoted by the limitation of arms and by the creation of the instrumentalities for peaceful settlement of controversies. But it will become a reality only through self-restraint and active effort in friendliness and helpfulness. I covet for this administration a record of having further contributed to advance the cause of peace.

Party Responsibilities

In our form of democracy the expression of the popular will can be effected only through the instrumentality of political parties. We maintain party government not to promote intolerant partisanship but because opportunity must be given for expression of the popular will, and organization provided for the execution of its mandates and for accountability of government to the people. It follows that the government both in the executive and the legislative branches must carry out in good faith the platforms upon which the party was entrusted with power. But the government is that of the whole people; the party is the instrument through which policies are determined and men chosen to bring them into being. The animosities of elections should have no place in our Government, for government must concern itself alone with the common weal.

Special Session of the Congress

Action upon some of the proposals upon which the Republican Party was returned to power, particularly further agricultural relief and limited changes in the tariff, cannot in justice to our farmers, our labor, and our manufacturers be postponed. I shall therefore request a special session of Congress for the consideration of these two questions. I shall deal with each of them upon the assembly of the Congress.

Other Mandates From The Election

It appears to me that the more important further mandates from the recent election were the maintenance of the integrity of the Constitution; the vigorous enforcement of the laws; the continuance of economy in public expenditure; the continued regulation of business to prevent domination in the community; the denial of ownership or operation of business by the Government in competition with its citizens; the avoidance of policies which would involve us in the controversies of foreign nations; the more effective reorganization of the departments of the Federal Government; the expansion of public works; and the promotion of welfare activities affecting education and the home.

These were the more tangible determinations of the election, but beyond them was the confidence and belief of the people that we would not neglect the support of the embedded ideals and aspirations of America. These ideals and aspirations are the touchstones upon which the day-to-day administration and legislative acts of government must be tested. More than this, the Government must, so far as lies within its proper powers, give leadership to the realization of these ideals and to the fruition of these aspirations. No one can adequately reduce these things of the spirit to phrases or to a catalogue of definitions. We do know what the attainments of these ideals should be: The preservation of self-government and its full foundations in local government; the perfection of justice whether in economic or in social fields; the maintenance of ordered liberty; the denial of domination by any group or class; the building up and preservation of equality of opportunity; the stimulation of initiative and individuality; absolute integrity in public affairs; the choice of officials for fitness to office; the direction of economic progress toward prosperity for the further lessening of poverty; the freedom of public opinion; the sustaining of education and of the advancement of knowledge; the growth of religious spirit and the tolerance of all faiths; the strengthening of the home; the advancement of peace.

There is no short road to the realization of these aspirations. Ours is a progressive people, but with a determination that progress must be based upon the foundation of experience. Ill-considered remedies for our faults bring only penalties after them. But if we hold the faith of the men in our mighty past who created these ideals, we shall leave them heightened and strengthened for our children.

Conclusion

This is not the time and place for extended discussion. The questions before our country are problems of progress to higher standards; they are not the problems of degeneration. They demand thought and they serve to quicken the conscience and enlist our sense of responsibility for their settlement. And that responsibility rests upon you, my countrymen, as much as upon those of us who have been selected for office.

Ours is a land rich in resources; stimulating in its glorious beauty; filled with millions of happy homes; blessed with comfort and opportunity. In no nation are the institutions of progress more advanced. In no nation are the fruits of accomplishment more secure. In no nation is the government more worthy of respect. No country is more loved by its people. I have an abiding faith in their capacity, integrity and high purpose. I have no fears for the future of our country. It is bright with hope.

In the presence of my countrymen, mindful of the solemnity of this occasion, knowing what the task means and the responsibility which it involves, I beg your tolerance, your aid, and your cooperation. I ask the help of Almighty God in this service to my country to which you have called me.

JAMES A. NELSON –
AUTHORS' PERSONAL NOTE

Young People: The story of President Herbert Hoover's Presidency is an example of the truth of the statement : "The

Victors initially write their version of History." In the First Edition of *"America's Opportunities",* I did not have a speech given by, or material about, President Herbert Hoover: Because of the Political Propaganda I had read, I believed that Inaction by Republican President Hoover's conservative Government created, sustained and even compounded the economic pain of The Great Depression of the 1930's. I was wrong !

Upon reading the Eugene Lyon biography about President Herbert Hoover's life, my view of this Great American President changed dramatically. It was very illuminating to learn that many of the Programs which blossomed during President Franklin Roosevelt's Administration were actually created during President Herbert Hoover's Administration: The Department of Veterans Affairs; The Reconstruction Finance Corporation (RFC); and the main parts of The National Recovery Administration (NRA); The Public Works Administration (PWA); and the Agricultural Adjustment Act (AAA).

During his long lifetime of service to his Country and the World, it is said by some Historians that Mr. Hoover and his loyal group of Associates with American Government Food Programs saved over two billion people from starvation. President Herbert Hoover, a man of God of the Quaker Faith, gave all of his Government Salary and Retirement Income to Charity. What a Great and God Filled American! We need a few more Citizens like him today ! All the World should never forget this extraordinary man, the 31st President of the United States Of America. (1929 – 1933).

PRESIDENT
FRANKLIN DELANO ROOSEVELT

Born: January 30, 1882
Died: March 29, 1945

MADISON SQUARE GARDEN ADDRESS

October 31, 1936

On the eve of a national election, it is well for us to stop for a moment and analyze calmly and without prejudice the effect on our Nation of a victory by either of the major political parties.

The problem of the electorate is far deeper, far more vital than the continuance in the Presidency of any individual. For the greater issue goes beyond units of humanity—it goes to humanity itself.

In 1932 the issue was the restoration of American democracy; and the American people were in a mood to win. They did win. In 1936 the issue is the preservation of their victory. Again they are in a mood to win. Again they will win.

More than four years ago in accepting the Democratic nomination in Chicago, I said: "Give me your help not to win votes alone, but to win in this crusade to restore America to its own people."

The banners of that crusade still fly in the van of a Nation that is on the march.

It is needless to repeat the details of the program which this Administration has been hammering out on the anvils of experience. No amount of misrepresentation or statistical contortion can conceal or blur or smear that record. Neither the attacks of unscrupulous enemies nor the exaggerations of over-zealous friends will serve to mislead the American people.

What was our hope in 1932? Above all other things the American people wanted peace. They wanted peace of mind instead of gnawing fear.

First, they sought escape from the personal terror which had stalked them for three years. They wanted the peace that comes from security in their homes: safety for their savings, permanence in their jobs, a fair profit from their enterprise.

Next, they wanted peace in the community, the peace that springs from the ability to meet the needs of community life: schools, playgrounds, parks, sanitation, highways—those things which are expected of solvent local government. They sought escape from disintegration and bankruptcy in local and state affairs.

They also sought peace within the Nation: protection of their currency, fairer wages, the ending of long hours of toil, the abolition of child labor, the elimination of wild-cat speculation, the safety of their children from kidnappers.

And, finally, they sought peace with other Nations— peace in a world of unrest. The Nation knows that I hate war, and I know that the Nation hates war.

I submit to you a record of peace; and on that record a well-founded expectation for future peace—peace for the individual, peace for the community, peace for the Nation, and peace with the world.

Tonight I call the roll—the roll of honor of those who stood with us in 1932 and still stand with us today.

Written on it are the names of millions who never had a chance—men at starvation wages, women in sweatshops, children at looms.

Written on it are the names of those who despaired, young men and young women for whom opportunity had become a will-o'-the-wisp.

Written on it are the names of farmers whose acres yielded only bitterness, business men whose books were portents of disaster, home owners who were faced with eviction, frugal citizens whose savings were insecure.

Written there in large letters are the names of countless other Americans of all parties and all faiths, Americans who had eyes to see and hearts to understand, whose consciences were burdened because too many of their fellows were burdened, who looked on these things four years ago and said, "This can be changed. We will change it."

We still lead that army in 1936. They stood with us then because in 1932 they believed. They stand with us today because in 1936 they know. And with them stand millions of new recruits who have come to know.

Their hopes have become our record.

We have not come this far without a struggle and I assure you we cannot go further without a struggle.

For twelve years this Nation was afflicted with hear-nothing, see-nothing, do-nothing Government. The Nation looked to Government but the Government looked away. Nine mocking years with the golden calf and three long years of the scourge! Nine crazy years at the ticker and three long years in the breadlines! Nine mad years of mirage and three

long years of despair! Powerful influences strive today to restore that kind of government with its doctrine that that Government is best which is most indifferent.

For nearly four years you have had an Administration which instead of twirling its thumbs has rolled up its sleeves. We will keep our sleeves rolled up.

We had to struggle with the old enemies of peace— business and financial monopoly, speculation, reckless banking, class antagonism, sectionalism, war profiteering.

They had begun to consider the Government of the United States as a mere appendage to their own affairs. We know now that Government by organized money is just as dangerous as Government by organized mob.

Never before in all our history have these forces been so united against one candidate as they stand today. They are unanimous in their hate for me—and I welcome their hatred.

I should like to have it said of my first Administration that in it the forces of selfishness and of lust for power met their match. I should like to have it said of my second Administration that in it these forces met their master.

The American people know from a four-year record that today there is only one entrance to the White House—by the front door. Since March 4, 1933, there has been only one pass-key to the White House. I have carried that key in my pocket. It is there tonight. So long as I am President, it will remain in my pocket.

Those who used to have pass-keys are not happy. Some of them are desperate. Only desperate men with their backs to the wall would descend so far below the level of decent citizenship as to foster the current pay-envelope campaign against America's working people. Only reckless men, heedless of consequences, would risk the disruption of the hope for a new peace between worker and employer by returning to the tactics of the labor spy.

Here is an amazing paradox! The very employers and politicians and publishers who talk most loudly of class antagonism and the destruction of the American system now undermine that system by this attempt to coerce the votes of the wage earners of this country. It is the 1936 version of the old threat to close down the factory or the office if a particular candidate does not win. It is an old strategy of tyrants to delude their victims into fighting their battles for them.

Every message in a pay envelope, even if it is the truth, is a command to vote according to the will of the employer. But this propaganda is worse—it is deceit.

They tell the worker his wage will be reduced by a contribution to some vague form of old-age insurance. They carefully conceal from him the fact that for every dollar of premium he pays for that insurance, the employer pays another dollar. That omission is deceit.

They carefully conceal from him the fact that under the federal law, he receives another insurance policy to help him if he loses his job, and that the premium of that policy is paid 100 percent by the employer and not one cent by the worker. They do not tell him that the insurance policy that is bought for him is far more favorable to him than any policy that any private insurance company could afford to issue. That omission is deceit.

They imply to him that he pays all the cost of both forms of insurance. They carefully conceal from him the fact that for every dollar put up by him his employer puts up three dollars three for one. And that omission is deceit.

But they are guilty of more than deceit. When they imply that the reserves thus created against both these policies will be stolen by some future Congress, diverted to some wholly foreign purpose, they attack the integrity and honor of American Government itself. Those who suggest that, are already aliens to the spirit of American democracy. Let them emigrate and try their lot under some foreign flag in which they have more confidence.

The fraudulent nature of this attempt is well shown by the record of votes on the passage of the Social Security Act. In addition to an overwhelming majority of Democrats in both Houses, seventy-seven Republican Representatives voted for it and only eighteen against it and fifteen Republican Senators voted for it and only five against it. Where does this last-minute drive of the Republican leadership leave these Republican Representatives and Senators who helped enact this law?

I am sure the vast majority of law-abiding businessmen who are not parties to this propaganda fully appreciate the extent of the threat to honest business contained in this coercion.

I have expressed indignation at this form of campaigning and I am confident that the overwhelming majority of employers, workers and the general public share that indignation and will show it at the polls on Tuesday next.

Aside from this phase of it, I prefer to remember this campaign not as bitter but only as hard-fought. There should be no bitterness or hate where the sole thought is the welfare of the United States of America. No man can occupy the office of President without realizing that he is President of all the people.

It is because I have sought to think in terms of the whole Nation that I am confident that today, just as four years ago, the people want more than promises.

Our vision for the future contains more than promises.

This is our answer to those who, silent about their own plans, ask us to state our objectives.

Of course we will continue to seek to improve working conditions for the workers of America—to reduce hours over-long, to increase wages that spell starvation, to end the labor of children, to wipe out sweatshops. Of course we will continue every effort to end monopoly in business, to support collective bargaining, to stop unfair competition, to abolish dishonorable trade practices. For all these we have only just begun to fight.

Of course we will continue to work for cheaper electricity in the homes and on the farms of America, for better and cheaper transportation, for low interest rates, for sounder home financing, for better banking, for the regulation of security issues, for reciprocal trade among nations, for the wiping out of slums. For all these we have only just begun to fight.

Of course we will continue our efforts in behalf of the farmers of America. With their continued cooperation we will do all in our power to end the piling up of huge surpluses which spelled ruinous prices for their crops. We will persist in successful action for better land use, for reforestation, for the conservation of water all the way from its source to the sea, for drought and flood control, for better marketing facilities for farm commodities, for a definite reduction of farm tenancy, for encouragement of farmer cooperatives, for crop insurance and a stable food supply. For all these we have only just begun to fight.

Of course we will provide useful work for the needy unemployed; we prefer useful work to the pauperism of a dole.

Here and now I want to make myself clear about those who disparage their fellow citizens on the relief rolls. They say that those on relief are not merely jobless—that they are worthless. Their solution for the relief problem is to end relief—to purge the rolls by starvation. To use the language of the stock broker, our needy unemployed would be cared for when, as, and if some fairy godmother should happen on the scene.

You and I will continue to refuse to accept that estimate of our unemployed fellow Americans. Your Government is still on the same side of the street with the Good Samaritan and not with those who pass by on the other side.

Again—what of our objectives?

Of course we will continue our efforts for young men and women so that they may obtain an education and an opportunity to put it to use. Of course we will continue our help for the crippled, for the blind, for the mothers, our insurance for the unemployed, our security for the

aged. Of course we will continue to protect the consumer against unnecessary price spreads, against the costs that are added by monopoly and speculation. We will continue our successful efforts to increase his purchasing power and to keep it constant.

For these things, too, and for a multitude of others like them, we have only just begun to fight.

All this—all these objectives—spell peace at home. All our actions, all our ideals, spell also peace with other nations.

Today there is war and rumor of war. We want none of it. But while we guard our shores against threats of war, we will continue to remove the causes of unrest and antagonism at home which might make our people easier victims to those for whom foreign war is profitable. You know well that those who stand to profit by war are not on our side in this campaign.

"Peace on earth, good will toward men"—democracy must cling to that message. For it is my deep conviction that democracy cannot live without that true religion which gives a nation a sense of justice and of moral purpose. Above our political forums, above our market places stand the altars of our faith—altars on which burn the fires of devotion that maintain all that is best in us and all that is best in our Nation.

We have need of that devotion today. It is that which makes it possible for government to persuade those who are mentally prepared to fight each other to go on instead, to work for and to sacrifice for each other. That is why we need to say with the Prophet: "What doth the Lord require of thee—but to do justly, to love mercy and to walk humbly with thy God." That is why the recovery we seek, the recovery we are winning, is more than economic. In it are included justice and love and humility, not for ourselves as individuals alone, but for our Nation.

That is the road to peace.

 # "THE ECONOMIC BILL OF RIGHTS"

January 11, 1944

Message to the Congress of the Unite States on the State of the Union

Excerpts From Speech:

It is our duty now to begin to lay the plans and determine the strategy for the winning of a lasting peace and the establishment of an American standard of living higher than ever before known. We cannot be content, no matter how high that general standard of living may be, if some fraction of our people— whether it be one-third or one-fifth or one-tenth—is ill-fed, ill-clothed, ill-housed, and insecure.

This Republic had its beginning, and grew to its present strength, under the protection of certain inalienable political rights—among them the right of free speech, free press, free worship, trial by jury, freedom from unreasonable searches and seizures. They were our rights to life and liberty.

As our nation has grown in size and stature, however—as our industrial economy expanded—these

political rights proved inadequate to assure us equality in the pursuit of happiness.

We have come to a clear realization of the fact that true individual freedom cannot exist without economic security and independence. "Necessitous men are not free men. People who are hungry and out of a job are the stuff of which dictatorships are made.

In our day these economic truths have become accepted as self-evident. We have accepted, so to speak, a second Bill of Rights under which a new basis of security and prosperity can be established for all—regardless of station, race, or creed.

Among these are:

The right to a useful and remunerative job in the industries or shops or farms or mines of the nation;

The right to earn enough to provide adequate food and clothing and recreation;

The right of every farmer to raise and sell his products at a return which will give him and his family a decent living;

The right of every businessman, large and small, to trade in an atmosphere of freedom from unfair competition and domination by monopolies at home or abroad;

The right of every family to a decent home;

The right to adequate medical care and the opportunity to achieve and enjoy good health;
The right to adequate protection from the economic fears of old age, sickness, accident, and unemployment;

The right to a good education.

All of these rights spell security. And after this <u>war</u> is won we must be prepared to move forward, in the implementation of these rights, to new goals of human happiness and well-being.

America's own rightful place in the world depends in large part upon how fully these and similar rights have been carried into practice for all our citizens.

For unless there is security here at home there cannot be lasting peace in the world.

PRESIDENT
HARRY S. TRUMAN

Born: May 8, 1884
Died: December 26, 1972

PROHIBITION OF
DISCRIMINATION IN THE MILITARY
EXECUTIVE ORDER

July 26,1948

" It is hereby declared to be the policy of the President that there shall be equality of treatment and opportunity for all persons in the armed services without regard to race, color, religion or national origin. This policy shall be put into effect as rapidly as possible, having due regard to the time required to effectuate any necessary changes without impairing efficiency or morale."

INAUGURAL ADDRESS AT THE US CAPITOL

January 20, 1949

Excerpts From Speech:

Mr. Vice President, Mr. Chief Justice, fellow citizens:

I accept with humility the honor which the American people have conferred upon me. I accept it with a resolve to do all that I can for the welfare of this Nation and for the peace of the world.

In performing the duties of my office, I need the help and the prayers of every one of you. I ask for your encouragement and for your support. The tasks we face are difficult. We can accomplish them only if we work together.

Each period of our national history has had its special challenges. Those that confront us now are as momentous as any in the past.

Today marks the beginning not only of a new administration, but of a period that will be eventful, perhaps decisive, for us and for the world.

It may be our lot to experience, and in a large measure bring about, a major turning point in the long history of the human race. The first half of this century has been marked by unprecedented and brutal attacks on the rights of man, and by the two most frightful wars in history. The supreme need of our time is for men to learn to live together in peace and harmony.

The peoples of the earth face the future with grave uncertainty, composed almost equally of great hopes and great fears. In this time of doubt, they look to the United States as never before for good will, strength, and wise leadership.

It is fitting, therefore, that we take this occasion to Proclaim to the world the essential principles of the faith by which we live, and to declare our aims to all peoples.

The American people stand firm in the faith which has inspired this Nation from the beginning. We believe that all men have a right to equal justice under law and equal opportunity to share in the common good. We believe that all men have a right to freedom of thought and expression. We believe that all men are created equal because they are created in the image of God.

From this faith we will not be moved.

The American people desire, and are determined to work for, a world in which all nations and all peoples are free to govern themselves as they see fit, and to achieve a decent and satisfying life. Above all else, our people desire, and are determined to work for, peace on earth-a just and lasting peace-based on genuine agreement freely arrived at by equals.

Democracy is based on the conviction that man has the moral and intellectual capacity, as well as the inalienable right, to govern himself with reason and justice.

Democracy maintains that government is established for the benefit of the individual, and is charged with the responsibility of protecting the rights of the individual and his freedom in the exercise of those abilities of his.

Democracy has proved that social justice can be achieved through peaceful change.

Democracy holds that free nations can settle differences justly and maintain a lasting peace.

Since the end of hostilities, the United States has invested its substance and its energy in a great constructive effort to restore peace, stability, and freedom to the world.

We have sought no territory. We have imposed our will on none. We have asked for no privileges we would not extend to others.

More than half the people of the world are living in conditions approaching misery. Their food is inadequate. They are victims of disease. Their economic life is primitive and stagnant. Their poverty is a handicap and a threat both to them and to more prosperous areas.

For the first time in history, humanity possesses the knowledge and skill to relieve the suffering of these people.

Our aim should be to help the free peoples of the world, through their own efforts, to produce more food, more clothing, more materials for housing, and more mechanical power to lighten their burdens.

Only by helping the least fortunate of its members to help themselves can the human family achieve the decent, satisfying life that is the right of all people.

Democracy alone can supply the vitalizing force to stir the peoples of the world into triumphant action, not only against their human oppressors, but also against their ancient enemies-hunger, misery, and despair.

We are aided by all who wish to live in freedom from fear-even by those who live today in fear under their own governments.

We are aided by all who want relief from lies and propaganda-those who desire truth and sincerity.

We are aided by all who desire self-government and a voice in deciding their own affairs.

We are aided by all who long for economic security-for the security and abundance that men in free societies can enjoy.

We are aided by all who desire freedom of speech, freedom of religion, and freedom to live their own lives for useful ends.

Our allies are the millions who hunger and thirst after righteousness.

In due time, as our stability becomes manifest, as more and more nations come to know the benefits of democracy and to participate in growing abundance. I believe that those countries which now oppose us will abandon their delusions and join with the free nations of the world in a just settlement of international differences

Events have brought our American democracy to new influence and new responsibilities. They will test our courage, our devotion to duty, and our concept of liberty.

But I say to all men, what we have achieved in liberty, we will surpass in greater liberty.

Steadfast in our faith in the Almighty, we will advance toward a world where man's freedom is secure.

To that end we will devote our strength, our resources, and our firmness of resolve. With God's help, the future of mankind will be assured in a world of justice, harmony, and peace.

"There is nothing new in the world except the history you do not Know."

President Harry S. Truman

PRESIDENT
DWIGHT D. EISENHOWER

Born: October 14, 1890
Died: March 28, 1969

MILITARY INDUSTRIAL COMPLEX SPEECH

January 17, 1961

My fellow Americans:

Three days from now, after half a century in the service of our country, I shall lay down the responsibilities of office as, in traditional and solemn ceremony, the authority of the Presidency is vested in my successor.

This evening I come to you with a message of leave-taking and farewell, and to share a few final thoughts with you, my countrymen.

Like every other citizen, I wish the new President, and all who will labor with him, Godspeed. I pray that the coming years will be blessed with peace and prosperity for all.

Our people expect their President and the Congress to find essential agreement on issues of great moment, the wise resolution of which will better shape the future of the Nation.

My own relations with the Congress, which began on a remote and tenuous basis when, long ago, a member of the Senate appointed me to West Point, have since ranged to the intimate during the war and immediate post-war period, and, finally, to the mutually interdependent during these past eight years.

In this final relationship, the Congress and the Administration have, on most vital issues, cooperated well, to serve the national good rather than mere partisanship, and so have assured that the business of the Nation should go forward. So, my official relationship with the Congress ends in a feeling, on my part, of gratitude that we have been able to do so much together.

We now stand ten years past the midpoint of a century that has witnessed four major wars among great nations. Three of these involved our own country. Despite these holocausts America is today the strongest, the most influential and most productive nation in the world. Understandably proud of this pre-eminence, we yet realize that America's leadership and prestige depend, not merely upon our unmatched material progress, riches and military strength, but on how we use our power in the interests of world peace and human betterment.

Throughout America's adventure in free government, our basic purposes have been to keep the peace; to foster progress in human achievement, and to enhance liberty, dignity and integrity among people and among nations. To strive for less would be unworthy of a free and religious people. Any failure traceable to arrogance, or our lack of comprehension or readiness to sacrifice would inflict upon us grievous hurt both at home and abroad.

Progress toward these noble goals is persistently threatened by the conflict now engulfing the world. It commands our whole attention, absorbs our very beings. We face a hostile ideology — global in scope, atheistic in character, ruthless in purpose, and insidious in method. Unhappily the danger is poses promises to be of indefinite duration. To meet it successfully, there is called for, not so much the emotional and transitory sacrifices of crisis, but rather those which enable us to carry forward steadily, surely, and without complaint the burdens of a prolonged and complex struggle — with liberty the stake. Only thus shall we remain, despite every provocation, on our charted course toward permanent peace and human betterment.

Crises there will continue to be. In meeting them, whether foreign or domestic, great or small, there is a recurring temptation to feel that some spectacular and costly action could become the miraculous solution to all current difficulties. A huge increase in newer elements of our defense; development of unrealistic programs to cure every ill in agriculture; a dramatic expansion in basic and

applied research — these and many other possibilities, each possibly promising in itself, may be suggested as the only way to the road we wish to travel.

But each proposal must be weighed in the light of a broader consideration: the need to maintain balance in and among national programs — balance between the private and the public economy, balance between cost and hoped for advantage — balance between the clearly necessary and the comfortably desirable; balance between our essential requirements as a nation and the duties imposed by the nation upon the individual; balance between actions of the moment and the national welfare of the future. Good judgment seeks balance and progress; lack of it eventually finds imbalance and frustration.

The record of many decades stands as proof that our people and their government have, in the main, understood these truths and have responded to them well, in the face of stress and threat. But threats, new in kind or degree, constantly arise. I mention two only.

A vital element in keeping the peace is our military establishment. Our arms must be mighty, ready for instant action, so that no potential aggressor may be tempted to risk his own destruction.

Our military organization today bears little relation to that known by any of my predecessors in peacetime, or indeed by the fighting men of World War II or Korea.

Until the latest of our world conflicts, the United States had no armaments industry. American makers of plowshares could, with time and as required, make swords as well. But now we can no longer risk emergency improvisation of national defense; we have been compelled to create a permanent armaments industry of vast proportions. Added to this, three and a half million men and women are directly engaged in the defense establishment. We annually spend on military security more than the net income of all United States corporations.

This conjunction of an immense military establishment and a large arms industry is new in the American experience. The total influence — economic, political, even spiritual — is felt in every city, every State house, every office of the Federal government. We recognize the imperative need for this development. Yet we must not fail to comprehend its grave implications. Our toil, resources and livelihood are all involved; so is the very structure of our society.

In the councils of government, we must guard against the acquisition of unwarranted influence, whether sought or unsought, by the military industrial complex. The potential for the disastrous rise of misplaced power exists and will persist.

We must never let the weight of this combination endanger our liberties or democratic processes. We should take nothing for granted. Only an alert and knowledgeable citizenry can compel the proper meshing of the huge industrial and military machinery of defense with our peaceful methods and goals, so that security and liberty may prosper together.

Akin to, and largely responsible for the sweeping changes in our industrial-military posture, has been the technological revolution during recent decades.

In this revolution, research has become central; it also becomes more formalized, complex, and costly. A steadily increasing share is conducted for, by, or at the direction of, the Federal government.

Today, the solitary inventor, tinkering in his shop, has been overshadowed by task forces of scientists in laboratories and testing fields. In the same fashion, the free university, historically the fountainhead of free ideas and scientific discovery, has experienced a revolution in the conduct of research. Partly because of the huge costs involved, a government contract becomes virtually a substitute for intellectual curiosity. For every old blackboard there are now hundreds of new electronic computers.

The prospect of domination of the nation's scholars by Federal employment, project allocations, and the power of money is ever present— and is gravely to be regarded.

Yet, in holding scientific research and discovery in respect, as we should, we must also be alert to the equal and opposite danger that public policy could itself become the captive of a scientific technological elite.

It is the task of statesmanship to mold, to balance, and to integrate these and other forces, new and old, within the principles of our democratic system — ever aiming toward the supreme goals of our free society.

Another factor in maintaining balance involves the element of time. As we peer into society's future, we — you and I, and our government — must avoid the impulse to live only for today, plundering, for our own ease and convenience, the precious resources of tomorrow. We cannot mortgage the material assets of our grandchildren without risking the loss also of their political and spiritual heritage. We want democracy to survive for all generations to come, not to become the insolvent phantom of tomorrow.

Down the long lane of the history yet to be written America knows that this world of ours, ever growing smaller, must avoid becoming a community of dreadful fear and hate, and be instead, a proud confederation of mutual trust and respect.

Such a confederation must be one of equals. The weakest must come to the conference table with the same confidence as do we, protected as we are by our moral, economic, and military strength. That table, though scarred by many past frustrations, cannot be abandoned for the certain agony of the battlefield.

Disarmament, with mutual honor and confidence, is a continuing imperative. Together we must learn how to compose differences, not with arms, but with intellect and decent purpose. Because this need is so sharp and apparent I confess that I lay down my official responsibilities in this field with a definite sense of disappointment. As one who has witnessed the horror and the lingering sadness of war — as one who knows that another war could utterly destroy this civilization which has been so slowly and painfully built over thousands of years — I wish I could say tonight that a lasting peace is in sight.

Happily, I can say that war has been avoided. Steady progress toward our ultimate goal has been made. But, so much remains to be done. As a private citizen, I shall never cease to do what little I can to help the world advance along that road.

So — in this my last good night to you as your President — I thank you for the many opportunities you have given me for public service in war and peace. I trust that in that service you find some things worthy; as for the rest of it, I know you will find ways to improve performance in the future.

You and I — my fellow citizens — need to be strong in our faith that all nations, under God, will reach the goal of peace with justice. May we be ever unswerving in devotion to principle, confident but humble with power, diligent in pursuit of the Nation's great goals.

To all the peoples of the world, I once more give expression to America's prayerful and continuing aspiration:

We pray that peoples of all faiths, all races, all nations, may have their great human needs satisfied; that those now denied opportunity shall come to enjoy it to the full; that all who yearn for freedom may experience its spiritual blessings; that those who have freedom will

understand, also, its heavy responsibilities; that all who are insensitive to the needs of others will learn charity; that the scourges of poverty, disease and ignorance will be made to disappear from the earth, and that, in the goodness of time, all peoples will come to live together in a peace guaranteed by the binding force of mutual respect and love.

Quotes From President Dwight D. Eisenhower:

I despise people who go to the gutter on either the right or the left and hurl rocks at those in the center.

* * *

There is nothing wrong with America that faith, love of freedom, intelligence, and energy of her citizens cannot cure.

* * *

The spirit of man is more important than mere physical strength, and the spiritual fiber of a nation than its wealth.

* * *

PRESIDENT
JOHN F. KENNEDY

Born: May 29, 1917
Assassinated: November 22, 1963

CIVIL RIGHTS SPEECH

June 11, 1963

Good evening, my fellow citizens:

This afternoon, following a series of threats and defiant statements, the presence of Alabama National Guardsmen was required on the University of Alabama to carry out the final and unequivocal order of the United States District Court of the Northern District of Alabama. That order called for the admission of two clearly qualified young Alabama residents who happened to have been born Negro. That they were admitted peacefully on the campus is due in good measure to the conduct of the students of the University of

Alabama, who met their responsibilities in a constructive way.

I hope that every American, regardless of where he lives, will stop and examine his conscience about this and other related incidents. This Nation was founded by men of many nations and backgrounds. It was founded on the principle that all men are created equal, and that the rights of every man are diminished when the rights of one man are threatened.

Today, we are committed to a worldwide struggle to promote and protect the rights of all who wish to be free. And when Americans are sent to Vietnam or West Berlin, we do not ask for whites only. It ought to be possible, therefore, for American students of any color to attend any public institution they select without having to be backed up by troops. It ought to to be possible for American consumers of any color to receive equal service in places of public accommodation, such as hotels and restaurants and theaters and retail stores, without being forced to resort to demonstrations in the street, and it ought to be possible for American citizens of any color to register and to vote in a free election without interference or fear of reprisal. It ought to to be possible, in short, for every American to enjoy the privileges of being American without regard to his race or his color. In short, every American ought to have the right to be treated as he would wish to be treated, as one would wish his children to be treated. But this is not the case.

The Negro baby born in America today, regardless of the section of the State in which he is born, has about one-half as much chance of completing a high school as a white baby born in the same place on the same day, one-third as much chance of completing college, one-third as much chance of becoming a professional man, twice as much chance of becoming unemployed, about one-seventh as much chance of earning $10,000 a year, a life expectancy which is 7 years shorter, and the prospects of earning only half as much.

This is not a sectional issue. Difficulties over segregation and discrimination exist in every city, in every State of the Union, producing in many cities a rising tide of discontent that threatens the public safety. Nor is this a partisan issue. In a time of domestic crisis men of good will and generosity should be able to unite regardless of party or politics. This is not even a legal or legislative issue alone. It is better to settle these matters in the courts than on the streets, and new laws are needed at every level, but law alone cannot make men see right. We are confronted primarily with a moral issue. It is as old as the Scriptures and is as clear as the American Constitution.

The heart of the question is whether all Americans are to be afforded equal rights and equal opportunities, whether we are going to treat our fellow Americans as we want to be treated. If an American, because his skin is dark, cannot eat lunch in a restaurant open to the public, if he cannot send his children to the best public school available, if he cannot vote for the public officials who will represent him, if, in short, he cannot enjoy the full and free life which all of us want, then who among us would be

content to have the color of his skin changed and stand in his place? Who among us would then be content with the counsels of patience and delay?

One hundred years of delay have passed since President Lincoln freed the slaves, yet their heirs, their grandsons, are not fully free. They are not yet freed from the bonds of injustice. They are not yet freed from social and economic oppression. And this Nation, for all its hopes and all its boasts, will not be fully free until all its citizens are free.

We preach freedom around the world, and we mean it, and we cherish our freedom here at home, but are we to say to the world, and much more importantly, to each other that this is the land of the free except for the Negroes; that we have no second-class citizens except Negroes; that we have no class or caste system, no ghettoes, no master race except with respect to Negroes?

Now the time has come for this Nation to fulfill its promise. The events in Birmingham and elsewhere have so increased the cries for equality that no city or State or legislative body can prudently choose to ignore them. The fires of frustration and discord are burning in every city, North and South, where legal remedies are not at hand. Redress is sought in the streets, in demonstrations, parades, and protests which create tensions and threaten violence and threaten lives.

We face, therefore, a moral crisis as a country and a people. It cannot be met by repressive police action. It cannot be left to increased demonstrations in the streets. It cannot be quieted by token moves or talk. It is a time to act in the

Congress, in your State and local legislative body and, above all, in all of our daily lives. It is not enough to pin the blame on others, to say this a problem of one section of the country or another, or deplore the facts that we face. A great change is at hand, and our task, our obligation, is to make that revolution, that change, peaceful and constructive for all. Those who do nothing are inviting shame, as well as violence. Those who act boldly are recognizing right, as well as reality.

Next week I shall ask the Congress of the United States to act, to make a commitment it has not fully made in this century to the proposition that race has no place in American life or law. The Federal judiciary has upheld that proposition in a series of forthright cases. The Executive Branch has adopted that proposition in the conduct of its affairs, including the employment of Federal personnel, the use of Federal facilities, and the sale of federally financed housing. But there are other necessary measures which only the Congress can provide, and they must be provided at this session. The old code of equity law under which we live commands for every wrong a remedy, but in too many communities, in too many parts of the country, wrongs are inflicted on Negro citizens and there are no remedies at law. Unless the Congress acts, their only remedy is the street.

I am, therefore, asking the Congress to enact legislation giving all Americans the right to be served in facilities which are open to the public — hotels, restaurants, theaters, retail stores, and similar establishments. This seems to me to be an elementary right. Its denial is an arbitrary indignity that no American in 1963 should have to endure, but many do.

I have recently met with scores of business leaders urging them to take voluntary action to end this discrimination, and I have been encouraged by their response, and in the last two weeks over 75 cities have seen progress made in desegregating these kinds of facilities. But many are unwilling to act alone, and for this reason, nationwide legislation is needed if we are to move this problem from the streets to the courts.

I'm also asking the Congress to authorize the Federal Government to participate more fully in lawsuits designed to end segregation in public education. We have succeeded in persuading many districts to desegregate voluntarily. Dozens have admitted Negroes without violence. Today, a Negro is attending a State-supported institution in every one of our 50 States, but the pace is very slow.

Too many Negro children entering segregated grade schools at the time of the Supreme Court's decision nine years ago will enter segregated high schools this fall, having suffered a loss which can never be restored. The lack of an adequate education denies the Negro a chance to get a decent job.

The orderly implementation of the Supreme Court decision, therefore, cannot be left solely to those who may not have the economic resources to carry the legal action or who may be subject to harassment.

Other features will be also requested, including greater protection for the right to vote. But legislation, I repeat, cannot solve this problem alone. It must be solved in the homes of every American in every community across our country. In this respect I wanna pay tribute to those citizens North and South who've been working in their communities to make life better for all. They are acting not out of sense of legal duty but out of a sense of human decency. Like our soldiers and sailors in all parts of the world they are meeting freedom's challenge on the firing line, and I salute them for their honor and their courage.

My fellow Americans, this is a problem which faces us all — in every city of the North as well as the South. Today, there are Negroes unemployed, two or three times as many compared to whites, inadequate education, moving into the large cities, unable to find work, young people particularly out of work without hope, denied equal rights, denied the opportunity to eat at a restaurant or a lunch counter or go to a movie theater, denied the right to a decent education, denied almost today the right to attend a State university even though qualified. It seems to me that these are matters which concern us all, not merely Presidents or Congressmen or Governors, but every citizen of the United States.

This is one country. It has become one country because all of us and all the people who came here had an equal chance to develop their talents. We cannot say to ten percent of the population that you can't have that right; that your children cannot have the chance to develop whatever talents they have; that the only way that they are going to get their rights

is to go in the street and demonstrate. I think we owe them and we owe ourselves a better country than that.

Therefore, I'm asking for your help in making it easier for us to move ahead and to provide the kind of equality of treatment which we would want ourselves; to give a chance for every child to be educated to the limit of his talents.

As I've said before, not every child has an equal talent or an equal ability or equal motivation, but they should have the equal right to develop their talent and their ability and their motivation, to make something of themselves.

We have a right to expect that the Negro community will be responsible, will uphold the law, but they have a right to expect that the law will be fair, that the Constitution will be color blind, as Justice Harlan said at the turn of the century.

This is what we're talking about and this is a matter which concerns this country and what it stands for, and in meeting it I ask the support of all our citizens.

Thank you very much.

PRESIDENT
LYNDON BAINES JOHNSON

Born: August 27, 1908
Died: January 22, 1973

CIVIL RIGHTS BILL

July 2, 1964

My fellow Americans:

I am about to sign into law the Civil Rights Act of 1964. I want to take this occasion to talk to you about what that law means to every American.

One hundred and eighty-eight years ago this week a small band of valiant men began a long struggle for freedom. They pledged their lives, their fortunes, and their sacred honor not only to found a nation, but to forge an ideal of freedom—not only for political independence, but for personal liberty—not only to eliminate foreign rule, but to establish the rule of justice in the affairs of men.

That struggle was a turning point in our history. Today in far corners of distant continents, the ideals of those American patriots still shape the struggles of men who hunger for freedom.

This is a proud triumph. Yet those who founded our country knew that freedom would be secure only if each generation fought to renew and enlarge its meaning. From the minutemen at Concord to the soldiers in Viet-Nam, each generation has been equal to that trust.

Americans of every race and color have died in battle to protect our freedom. Americans of every race and color have worked to build a nation of widening opportunities. Now our generation of Americans has been called on to continue the unending search for justice within our own borders.

We believe that all men are created equal. Yet many are denied equal treatment.

We believe that all men have certain unalienable rights. Yet many Americans do not enjoy those rights.

We believe that all men are entitled to the blessings of liberty. Yet millions are being deprived of those blessings — not because of their own failures, but because of the color of their skin.

The reasons are deeply imbedded in history and tradition and the nature of man. We can understand—without rancor or hatred—how this all happened.

But it cannot continue. Our Constitution, the foundation of our Republic, forbids it. The principles of our freedom forbid it. Morality forbids it. And the law I will sign tonight forbids it.

That law is the product of months of the most careful debate and discussion. It was proposed more than one year ago by our late and beloved President John F. Kennedy. It received the bipartisan support of more than two-thirds of the Members of both the House and the Senate. An overwhelming majority of Republicans as well as Democrats voted for it.

It has received the thoughtful support of tens of thousands of civic and religious leaders in all parts of this Nation. And it is supported by the great majority of the American people.

The purpose of the law is simple.

It does not restrict the freedom of any American, so long as he respects the rights of others.

It does not give special treatment to any citizen.

It does say the only limit to a man's hope for happiness, and for the future of his children, shall be his own ability.

210

It does say that there are those who are equal before God shall now also be equal in the polling booths, in the classrooms, in the factories, and in hotels, restaurants, movie theaters, and other places that provide service to the public.

I am taking steps to implement the law under my constitutional obligation to "take care that the laws are faithfully executed."

We must not approach the observance and enforcement of this law in a vengeful spirit. Its purpose is not to punish. Its purpose is not to divide, but to end divisions—divisions which have all lasted too long. Its purpose is national, not regional.

Its purpose is to promote a more abiding commitment to freedom, a more constant pursuit of justice, and a deeper respect for human dignity

We will achieve these goals because most Americans are law-abiding citizens who want to do what is right.

This is why the Civil Rights Act relies first on voluntary compliance, then on the efforts of local communities and States to secure the rights of citizens. It provides for the national authority to step in only when others cannot or will not do the job.

This Civil Rights Act is a challenge to all of us to go to work in our communities and our States, in our homes and in our hearts, to eliminate the last vestiges of injustice in our beloved country.

So tonight I urge every public official, every religious leader, every business and professional man, every workingman, every housewife—I urge every American—to join in this effort to bring justice and hope to all our people—and to bring peace to our land.

My fellow citizens, we have come now to a time of testing. We must not fail.

Let us close the springs of racial poison. Let us pray for wise and understanding hearts. Let us lay aside irrelevant differences and make our Nation whole. Let us hasten that day when our unmeasured strength and our unbounded spirit will be free to do the great works ordained for this Nation by the just and wise God who is the Father of us all.

Thank you and good night.

 # VOTING RIGHTS ACT ADDRESS

March 15, 1965

I speak tonight for the dignity of man and the destiny of democracy.

I urge every member of both parties—Americans of all religions and of all colors—from every section of this country—to join me in that cause.

At times history and fate meet at a single time in a single place to shape a turning point in man's unending search for freedom. So it was at Lexington and Concord. So it was a century ago at Appomattox. So it was last week in Selma, Alabama.

There is no Negro problem. There is no southern problem. There is no northern problem. There is only an American problem.

And we are met here tonight as Americans—not as Democrats or Republicans—we are met here as Americans to solve that problem.

This was the first nation in the history of the world to be founded with a purpose. The great phrases of that purpose still sound in every American heart, north and south: "All men are created equal" — "Government by consent of the governed" — "Give me liberty or give me death."...

Those words are a promise to every citizen that he shall share in the dignity of man. This dignity cannot be found in man's possessions. It cannot be found in his power or in his position. It really rests on his right to be treated as a man equal in opportunity to all others. It says that he shall share in freedom, he shall choose his leaders, educate his children, provide for his family according to his ability and his merits as a human being....

Many of the issues of civil rights are very complex and most difficult. But about this there can and should be no argument. Every American citizen must have an equal right to vote. There is no reason which can excuse the denial of that right. There is no duty which weighs more heavily on us than the duty we have to ensure that right.

Yet the harsh fact is that in many places in this country men and women are kept from voting simply because they are Negroes....

Experience has clearly shown that the existing process of law cannot overcome systematic and ingenious discrimination. No law that we now have on the books— and I have helped to put three of them there—can ensure the right to vote when local officials are determined to deny it.

In such a case our duty must be clear to all of us. The Constitution says that no person shall be kept from voting because of his race or his color. We have all sworn an oath before God to support and to defend that Constitution.

We must now act in obedience to that oath.

Wednesday I will send to Congress a law designed to eliminate illegal barriers to the right to vote....

To those who seek to avoid action by their National Government in their home communities—who want to and who seek to maintain purely local control over elections— the answer is simple. Open your polling places to all your people. Allow men and women to register and vote whatever the color of their skin. Extend the rights of citizenship to every citizen of this land. There is no constitutional issue here. The command of the Constitution is plain. There is no moral issue. It is wrong—deadly wrong—to deny any of your fellow Americans the right to vote in this country. There is no issue of States rights or National rights. There is only the struggle for human rights.

I have not the slightest doubt what will be your answer....

But even if we pass this bill, the battle will not be over. What happened in Selma is part of a far larger movement

which reaches into every section and State of America. It is the effort of American Negroes to secure for themselves the full blessings of American life.

Their cause must be our cause too, because it is not just Negroes but really it is all of us, who must overcome the crippling legacy of bigotry and injustice. And we shall overcome...

This great, rich, restless country can offer opportunity and education and hope to all—all black and white, all North and South, sharecropper and city dweller. These are the enemies—poverty, ignorance, disease—they are our enemies, not our fellow man, not our neighbor. And these enemies too—poverty, disease, and ignorance—we shall overcome.

PRESIDENT
RONALD W. REAGAN

Born: February 6, 1911
Died: June 5, 2004

FAREWELL ADDRESS TO THE NATION

January 11, 1989

on Television from the Oval Office

Excerpts From Speech:

It's been quite a journey this decade, and we held together through some stormy seas. And at the end, together, we are reaching our destination.

The fact is, from Grenada to the Washington and Moscow summits, from the recession of '81 to '82, to the expansion that began in late '82 and continues to this day, we've made a difference. The way I see it, there were two great triumphs, two things that I'm proudest of. One is the economic recovery, in which the people of America created—and filled—19 million new jobs. The other is the recovery of our morale. America is respected again in the world and looked to for leadership.

Well, back in 1980, when I was running for President, it was all so different. Some pundits said our programs would result in catastrophe. Our views on foreign affairs would cause war. Our plans for the economy would cause inflation to soar and bring about economic collapse. I even remember one highly respected economist saying, back in 1982, that "The engines of economic growth have shut down here, and they're likely to stay that way for years to come." Well, he and the other opinion leaders were wrong. The fact is what they call "radical" was really "right." What they called "dangerous" was just "desperately needed."

And in all of that time I won a nickname, "The Great Communicator." But I never thought it was my style or the words I used that made a difference: it was the content. I wasn't a great communicator, but I communicated great things, and they didn't spring full bloom from my brow, they came from the heart of a great nation—from our experience, our wisdom, and our belief in the principles that have guided us for two centuries. They called it the Reagan revolution. Well, I'll accept that, but for me it always seemed more like the great rediscovery, a rediscovery of our values and our common sense.

Common sense told us that when you put a big tax on something, the people will produce less of it. So, we cut the people's tax rates, and the people produced more than ever before. The economy bloomed like a plant that had been cut back and could now grow quicker and stronger. Our economic program brought about the longest peacetime expansion in our history: real family income up, the poverty rate down, entrepreneurship booming, and an explosion in research and new technology. We're exporting more than ever because American industry became more competitive, and at the same time, we summoned the national will to knock down protectionist walls abroad instead of erecting them at home.

Common sense also told us that to preserve the peace, we'd have to become strong again after years of weakness and confusion. So, we rebuilt our defenses, and this New Year we toasted the new peacefulness around the globe. Not only have the superpowers actually begun to reduce their stockpiles of nuclear weapons—and hope for even more progress is bright—but the regional conflicts that rack the globe are also beginning to cease. The Persian Gulf is no longer a war zone. The Soviets are leaving Afghanistan. The Vietnamese are preparing to pull out of Cambodia, and an American-mediated accord will soon send 50,000 Cuban troops home from Angola.

The lesson of all this was, of course, that because we're a great nation, our challenges seem complex. It will always be this way. But as long as we remember our first principles and believe in ourselves, the future will always be ours. And something else we learned: Once you begin a great movement, there's no telling where it will end. We meant to change a nation, and instead, we changed a world.

When you've got to the point when you can celebrate the anniversaries of your 39th birthday, you can sit back sometimes, review your life, and see it flowing before you. For me there was a fork in the river, and it was right in the middle of my life. I never meant to go into politics. It wasn't my intention when I was young. But I was raised to believe you had to pay your way for the blessings bestowed on you. I was happy with my career in the entertainment world, but I ultimately went into politics because I wanted to protect something precious.

Ours was the first revolution in the history of mankind that truly reversed the course of government, and with three little words: "We the People." "We the People" tell the government what to do; it doesn't tell us. "We the People" are the driver; the government is the car. And we decide where it should go, and by what route, and how fast. Almost all the world's constitutions are documents in which governments tell the people what their privileges are. Our Constitution is a document in which "We the People" tell the government what it is allowed to do. "We the People" are free. This belief has been the underlying basis for everything I've tried to do these past 8 years.

But back in the 1960's, when I began, it seemed to me that we'd begun reversing the order of things — that through more and more rules and regulations and confiscatory taxes, the government was taking more of our money, more of our options, and more of our freedom. I went into politics in part to put up my hand and say, "Stop." I was a citizen politician, and it seemed the right thing for a citizen to do.

I think we have stopped a lot of what needed stopping. And I hope we have once again reminded people that man is not free unless government is limited. There's a clear cause and effect here that is as neat and predictable as a law of physics: As government expands, liberty contracts.

I've been asked if I have any regrets. Well, I do. The deficit is one. I've been talking a great deal about that lately, but tonight isn't for arguments, and I'm going to hold my tongue. But an observation: I've had my share of victories in the Congress, but what few people noticed is that I never won anything you didn't win for me. They never saw my troops, they never saw Reagan's regiments, the American people. You won every battle with every call you made and letter you wrote demanding action. Well, action is still needed. If we're to finish the job. Reagan's regiments will have to become the Bush brigades. Soon he'll be the chief, and he'll need you every bit as much as I did.

Finally, there is a great tradition of warnings in Presidential farewells, and I've got one that's been on my mind for some time. But oddly enough, it starts with one of the things I'm proudest of in the past 8 years: the resurgence of national pride that I called the new patriotism. This national feeling is good, but it won't count for much, and it won't last unless it's grounded in thoughtfulness and knowledge.

An informed patriotism is what we want. And are we doing a good enough job teaching our children what America is and what she represents in the long history of the world? Those of us who are over 35 or so years of age grew up in a different America. We were taught, very directly, what it means to be an

American. And we absorbed, almost in the air, a love of country and an appreciation of its institutions. If you didn't get these things from your family, you got them from the neighborhood, from the father down the street who fought in Korea or the family who lost someone at Anzio. Or you could get a sense of patriotism from school. And if all else failed, you could get a sense of patriotism from the popular culture. The movies celebrated democratic values and implicitly reinforced the idea that America was special. TV was like that, too, through the mid-sixties.

But now, we're about to enter the nineties, and some things have changed. Younger parents aren't sure that an un-ambivalent appreciation of America is the right thing to teach modern children. And as for those who create the popular culture, well-grounded patriotism is no longer the style. Our spirit is back, but we haven't re-institutionalized it. We've got to do a better job of getting across that America is freedom— freedom of speech, freedom of religion, freedom of enterprise. And freedom is special and rare. It's fragile; it needs protection.

So, we've got to teach history based not on what's in fashion but what's important—why the Pilgrims came here, who Jimmy Doolittle was, and what those 30 seconds over Tokyo meant. You know, 4 years ago on the 40th anniversary of D-Day, I read a letter from a young woman writing to her late father, who'd fought on Omaha Beach. Her name was Lisa Zanatta Henn, and she said, "We will always remember, we will never forget what the boys of Normandy did." Well, let's help her keep her word. If we forget what we did, we won't know who we are. I'm warning of an eradication of the American memory that could result, ultimately, in an erosion of the American spirit. Let's start with some basics: more attention to American history and a greater emphasis on civic ritual.

And let me offer lesson number one about America: All great change in America begins at the dinner table. So, tomorrow night in the kitchen, I hope the talking begins. And children, if your parents haven't been teaching you what it means to be an American, let 'em know and nail 'em on it. That would be a very American thing to do.

And that's about all I have to say tonight, except for one thing. The past few days when I've been at that window upstairs, I've thought a bit of the "shining city upon a hill." The phrase comes from John Winthrop, who wrote it to describe the America he imagined. What he imagined was important because he was an early Pilgrim, an early freedom man. He journeyed here on what today we'd call a little wooden boat; and like the other Pilgrims, he was looking for a home that would be free. I've spoken of the shining city all my political life, but I don't know if I ever quite communicated what I saw when I said it. But in my mind it was a tall, proud city built on rocks stronger than oceans, windswept, God-blessed, and teeming with people of all kinds living in harmony and peace; a city with free ports that hummed with commerce and creativity. And if there had to be city walls, the walls had doors and the doors were open to anyone with the will and the heart to get here. That's how I saw it, and see it still.

And how stands the city on this winter night? More prosperous, more secure, and happier than it was 8 years ago. But more than that: After 200 years, two centuries, she still stands strong and true on the granite ridge, and her glow has held steady no matter what storm. And she's still a beacon, still a magnet for all who must have freedom, for all the pilgrims from all the lost places who are hurtling through the darkness, toward home.

And so, goodbye, God bless you, and God bless the United States of America.

PRESIDENT
JOHN F. KENNEDY

 ## MOON SPEECH

September 12, 1962

At Rice University, Houston Texas

I appreciate your president having made me an honorary visiting professor, and I will assure you that my first lecture will be very brief.

I am delighted to be here, and I'm particularly delighted to be here on this occasion.

We meet at a college noted for knowledge, in a city noted for progress, in a State noted for strength, and we stand in need of all three, for we meet in an hour of change and challenge, in a decade of hope and fear, in an age of both knowledge and ignorance. The greater our knowledge increases, the greater our ignorance unfolds.

Despite the striking fact that most of the scientists that the world has ever known are alive and working today, despite the fact that this Nation's own scientific manpower is doubling every 12 years in a rate of growth more than three times that of our population as a whole, despite that, the vast stretches of the unknown and the unanswered and the unfinished still far outstrip our collective comprehension.

No man can fully grasp how far and how fast we have come, but condense, if you will, the 50,000 years of man's recorded history in a time span of but a half-century. Stated in these terms, we know very little about the first 40 years, except at the end of them advanced man had learned to use the skins of animals to cover them. Then about 10 years ago, under this standard, man emerged from his caves to construct other kinds of shelter. Only five years ago man learned to write and use a cart with wheels. Christianity began less than two years ago. The printing press came this year, and then less than two months ago, during this whole 50-year span of human history, the steam engine provided a new source of power.

Newton explored the meaning of gravity. Last month electric lights and telephones and automobiles and airplanes became available. Only last week did we develop penicillin and television and nuclear power, and now if America's new spacecraft succeeds in reaching Venus, we will have literally reached the stars before midnight tonight.

This is a breathtaking pace, and such a pace cannot help but create new ills as it dispels old, new ignorance, new problems, new dangers. Surely the opening vistas of space promise high costs and hardships, as well as high reward.

So it is not surprising that some would have us stay where we are a little longer to rest, to wait. But this city of Houston, this State of Texas, this country of the United States was not built by those who waited and rested and wished to look behind them. This country was conquered by those who moved forward—and so will space.

William Bradford, speaking in 1630 of the founding of the Plymouth Bay Colony, said that all great and honorable actions are accompanied with great difficulties, and both must be enterprised and overcome with answerable courage.

If this capsule history of our progress teaches us anything, it is that man, in his quest for knowledge and progress, is determined and cannot be deterred. The exploration of space will go ahead, whether we join in it or not, and it is one of the great adventures of all time, and no nation which expects to be the leader of other nations can expect to stay behind in the race for space.

Those who came before us made certain that this country rode the first waves of the industrial revolutions, the first waves of modern invention, and the first wave of nuclear power, and this generation does not intend to founder in the backwash of the coming age of space. We mean to be a part of it—we mean to lead it. For the eyes of the world now look into space, to the moon and to the planets beyond, and we have vowed that we shall not see it governed by a hostile flag of conquest, but by a banner of freedom and peace. We have vowed that we shall not see space filled with weapons of mass destruction, but with instruments of knowledge and understanding.

Yet the vows of this Nation can only be fulfilled if we in this Nation are first, and, therefore, we intend to be first. In short, our leadership in science and in industry, our hopes for peace and security, our obligations to ourselves as well as others, all require us to make this effort, to solve these mysteries, to solve them for the good of all men, and to become the world's leading space-faring nation.

We set sail on this new sea because there is new knowledge to be gained, and new rights to be won, and they must be won and used for the progress of all people. For space science, like nuclear science and all technology, has no conscience of its own. Whether it will become a force for good or ill depends on man, and only if the United States occupies a position of pre-eminence can we help decide whether this new ocean will be a sea of peace or a new terrifying theater of war. I do not say the we should or will go unprotected against the hostile misuse of space any more than we go unprotected against the hostile use of land or sea, but I do say that space can be explored and mastered without feeding the fires of war, without repeating the mistakes that man has made in extending his writ around this globe of ours.

There is no strife, no prejudice, no national conflict in outer space as yet. Its hazards are hostile to us all. Its conquest deserves the best of all mankind, and its opportunity for peaceful cooperation many never come again. But why, some say, the moon? Why choose this as our goal? And they may well ask why climb the highest mountain? Why, 35 years ago, fly the Atlantic? Why does Rice play Texas?

We choose to go to the moon. We choose to go to the moon in this decade and do the other things, not because they are easy, but because they are hard, because that goal will serve to organize and measure the best of our energies and skills, because that challenge is one that we are willing to accept, one we are unwilling to postpone, and one which we intend to win, and the others, too.

It is for these reasons that I regard the decision last year to shift our efforts in space from low to high gear as among the most important decisions that will be made during my incumbency in the office of the Presidency.

In the last 24 hours we have seen facilities now being created for the greatest and most complex exploration in man's history. We have felt the ground shake and the air shattered by the testing of a Saturn C-1 booster rocket, many times as powerful as the Atlas which launched John Glenn, generating power equivalent to 10,000 automobiles with their accelerators on the floor. We have seen the site where the F-1 rocket engines, each one as powerful as all eight engines of the Saturn combined, will be clustered together to make the advanced Saturn missile, assembled in a new building to be built at Cape Canaveral as tall as a 48 story structure, as wide as a city block, and as long as two lengths of this field.

Within these last 19 months at least 45 satellites have circled the earth. Some 40 of them were "made in the United States of America" and they were far more sophisticated and supplied far more knowledge to the people of the world than those of the Soviet Union.

The Mariner spacecraft now on its way to Venus is the most intricate instrument in the history of space science. The accuracy of that shot is comparable to firing a missile from Cape Canaveral and dropping it in this stadium between the the 40-yard lines.

Transit satellites are helping our ships at sea to steer a safer course. Tiros satellites have given us unprecedented warnings of hurricanes and storms, and will do the same for forest fires and icebergs.

We have had our failures, but so have others, even if they do not admit them. And they may be less public.

To be sure, we are behind, and will be behind for some time in manned flight. But we do not intend to stay behind, and in this decade, we shall make up and move ahead.

The growth of our science and education will be enriched by new knowledge of our universe and environment, by new techniques of learning and mapping and observation, by new tools and computers for industry, medicine, the home as well as the school. Technical institutions, such as Rice, will reap the harvest of these gains.

And finally, the space effort itself, while still in its infancy, has already created a great number of new companies, and tens of thousands of new jobs. Space and related industries are generating new demands in investment and skilled personnel, and this city and this State, and this region, will share greatly in this growth. What was once the furthest outpost on the old frontier of the West will be the furthest outpost on the new frontier of science and space. Houston, your City of Houston, with its Manned Spacecraft Center, will become the heart of a large scientific and engineering community. During the next 5 years the National Aeronautics and Space Administration expects to double the number of scientists and engineers in this area, to increase its outlays for salaries and expenses to

$60 million a year; to invest some $200 million in plant and laboratory facilities; and to direct or contract for new space efforts over $1 billion from this Center in this City.

To be sure, all this costs us all a good deal of money. This year's space budget is three times what it was in January 1961, and it is greater than the space budget of the previous eight years combined. That budget now stands at $5,400 million a year—a staggering sum, though somewhat less than we pay for cigarettes and cigars every year. Space expenditures will soon rise some more, from 40 cents per person per week to more than 50 cents a week for every man, woman and child in the United Stated, for we have given this program a high national priority—even though I realize that this is in some measure an act of faith and vision, for we do not now know what benefits await us.

But if I were to say, my fellow citizens, that we shall send to the moon, 240,000 miles away from the control station in Houston, a giant rocket more than 300 feet tall, the length of this football field, made of new metal alloys, some of which have not yet been invented, capable of standing heat and stresses several times more than have ever been experienced, fitted together with a precision better than the finest watch, carrying all the equipment needed for propulsion, guidance, control, communications, food and survival, on an untried mission, to an unknown celestial body, and then return it safely to earth, re-entering the atmosphere at speeds of over 25,000 miles per hour, causing heat about half that of the temperature of the sun—almost as hot as it is here today—and do all this, and do it right, and do it first before this decade is out—then we must be bold.

I'm the one who is doing all the work, so we just want you to stay cool for a minute. [laughter]

However, I think we're going to do it, and I think that we must pay what needs to be paid. I don't think we ought to waste any money, but I think we ought to do the job. And this will be done in the decade of the sixties. It may be done while some of you are still here at school at this college and university. It will be done during the term of office of some of the people who sit here on this platform. But it will be done. And it will be done before the end of this decade.

I am delighted that this university is playing a part in putting a man on the moon as part of a great national effort of the United States of America.

Many years ago the great British explorer George Mallory, who was to die on Mount Everest, was asked why did he want to climb it. He said, "Because it is there."

Well, space is there, and we're going to climb it, and the moon and the planets are there, and new hopes for knowledge and peace are there. And, therefore, as we set sail we ask God's blessing on the most hazardous and dangerous and greatest adventure on which man has ever embarked.

Thank you.

YOUNG PEOPLE

You are challenged with turning around this Great Ship Of State: The United States Of America. We are a Country which by the words of our Constitution is "By The People, Of The People, and For The People." We are a Country known as the Land of The Free and The Home of the Brave. We are also a Country which is supposed to be dedicated to equality, fairness and opportunity for all Americans: Unfortunately for many Americans today, this is not the case.

In the almost seventy years since the end of World War II, The United States has become something other than what our Founders envisioned. Today 20 per cent of our people own 89 per cent of our private wealth. Almost two million of our population are incarcerated; many of our Citizens currently are unemployed or under-employed and, most perilous of all risks we face, The United States Of America is now staggering economically under almost 20 trillion dollars of National Debt.

Young People, you must educate yourselves about the issues; then, work diligently to create solutions to America's problems for the good of all Americans. You must stay the course until sound legislative programs are in place to help as many citizens as possible while hurting as few as possible. Those who can afford to pay more in taxes **must**; those who are the most vulnerable of our society **must** be protected as much as possible against human misery caused by economic or physical hardship. **You must elect Leaders who will work in behalf of All Americans, not just a privileged few.**

Americans are not lazy. Working Americans want and need a job that pays a living wage income with health benefits. Fools who suggest otherwise are just that: **Fools!** Sufficient employment to provide sustenance for an individual or a Family must be available for all working Americans.

Young people, you are following older Americans who have let their Government make horrible economic mistakes through, **One**, using National Treasure in the Wars of other Countries which did not threaten our National Security; **Two**, by using taxpayer money to make Wall Street Robber Barons financially whole after their Companies lost millions of dollars on disastrous home mortgage loans. **Three,** by allowing Corporations to function like individual citizens, buying and selling Politicians through disgusting, odious election contributions. **These very costly mistakes were the results of dangerous leadership hubris in the first instance and business greed in the second and third.**

Young people, you must work to pass tough laws which will threaten Wall Street thieves with long jail terms and massive economic fines for stock market and banking chicanery which could quickly destroy the financial and social life of the United States. You must keep our glorious Military at home where it belongs, out of harm's way, unless our National Security is truly at stake. Throughout our history, many outstanding Presidents and Professional Military Leaders have cautioned us about making such costly and foolish mistakes. Finally, you must pass a law to once and for all, declare a Corporation is not and does not have the Constitutional right of a United States Citizen. To paraphrase priceless wisdom, a smart person (probably a Woman) once said, "Re-Election Insanity is making the same voting mistake over and over again, while expecting a different Legislative Result."

For too long the Electorate has been acting like Idiots: Voting Leaders who just take orders from the rich top twenty percent and their lobbyists, while the bottom eighty percent of the population suffer economically.

Please, **Young People**, act with greater National Intelligence, Creativity and Courage than those who have lived before you; undoubtedly, The United States and the entire World will be the better for it.

Young People, some political charlatans and media pundits want you to think the United States Of America is on a downhill path to match the Roman Empire: Nothing could be further from the truth! Do not just take my words for proof — read Roman History. America is a Republic with elected officials and Constitutionally Proclaimed Equal Rights For All Citizens; Rome was a republic whose citizens did not have equal rights and whose government was an absolute monarchy, led by an Emperor.

Our Government exists to serve its people by fostering freedom and prosperity for all; the Roman Empire existed to subjugate many of its people and create prosperity for a few. The Roman Empire thrived by brute force and murder. As momentous and horrific as the Crucifixion of Jesus Christ was, Our Lord was certainly not the only person killed during the reign of the Roman Empire.

The Roman Legion existed to conquer, control and enslave the subjects of the Roman Empire. Our US Military from The Continental Army under General George Washington to the present has been used, First, to obtain our freedom from England and, Second, to maintain our freedom against the likes of Hitler and the Nazis and ToJo and the Japanese. The United States Of America has never used its Military to fight wars to enslave our enemies. Instead, after the conflict was over, America has always spent millions of dollars to help defeated and impoverished Countries return to a life of Peace, Prosperity and Freedom; and our Military has always played an important role in the re-development.

During my lifetime, it is true that America has had its share of horrible incidents of Government Mistreatment of Citizens: The Japanese-American Internment Camps during World War II, The Kent State Student Shooting During The Viet Nam War, Ruby Ridge, The Waco Siege Of The

Religious Group Branch Davidian and police brutality, such as the inexcusable beating of Mr. Rodney King. But, most of our history of internal conflict has involved the gallant story of The American Negro's Heroic Fight For Civil Rights and Labor/Management Confrontations over the Economic Conditions of American Workers.

I have purposely positioned President John F. Kennedy's *Moon Speech* last in *"America's Opportunities."* The *Moon Speech* is a living reminder of what the great people of The United States can accomplish when American Will And Purpose are joined with American Minds, Human Energy, and Taxpayer Money to meet an important and very serious National Challenge.

Finally, you must always remember that The United States is "One Nation Under God." GOD is our Great Protector; Our Ultimate Answer In Times Of National Trial And Tribulation. You must Never Forget The Power Of Prayer; And May You Always Know The Omnipotent, Gracious Love of God.

May God Bless You In Your Future Work,
Jim.

May you NEVER forget what Former President Harry S. Truman said:

"There is nothing new in the world except the History you do not know."

Read, Young People, READ.

2014

Dear God,

Thank you for my beautiful Family that you have given me: my wife, Marylil; my four children, Sabryna Apollo Bach, Darrick James Martin Nelson, Vanessa Angelica McCalister, and Tyrone Forrest Nelson; and my grandson, Tyler Darrick Nelson. May we love and support each other as long as YOU give us life.

Thank you for this great Nation in which we live: the United States of America. Even with all of our imperfections, it is still the greatest Country in the world. Please grant us a safe and sure path through our current economic and political turmoil.

Let us always help others as we help ourselves. Let us as well use our diplomatic powers of persuasion before we employ our military might.

I pray, Dear God, that You will guide us to use wisdom and fairness to help right the wrongs of the world as well as those within our own Country. Please help us to always remember that if we destroy ourselves in the process, we have helped no one.

*Please grant us the intelligence and good luck to elect leaders who will always act in the best interest of **ALL** Americans. Please allow us to acknowledge that governing is not as easy as it may appear from the outside looking in; Please allow us to remember that our government is challenging at best.*

Let us pray that petty political party differences, sectional disputes and religious objections can be overcome to solve our nation's most pressing problems - above all, our almost twenty – trillion—dollar debt.

Amen.

James A. Nelson

BUDDY NELSON'S HANGAR is as big
as man's imagination. There are no locks
on the doors and the only membership
requirements are Curiosity, Faith, Desire
and Determination.

Jim and Yokie

Jim and Yokie - - A Great Pyrenees rescued by Jim in the State of Wyoming

Yokie is now waiting for Jim at Rainbow Bridge

www.ingramcontent.com/pod-product-compliance
Lightning Source LLC
Chambersburg PA
CBHW070851290526
45795CB00001B/75